Praise for *Plant Like Jesus*

Plant Like Jesus is a book that I know will hit home for a lot of church plant-ers. It did with me! Planting a church is one of the hardest things you can do as a pastor. It's easy to lean only on strategy and not enough on Jesus. This book of devotionals for the church planter puts the focus back where it needs to be and should have been all along: on Jesus.

—**Adam Weber**, lead pastor of Embrace Church
and author of *Talking with God*

In *Plant Like Jesus*, Ben Ingebretson offers spiritual food for the soul of any-one planting a new church, starting a new ministry, or contemplating what it looks like to reclaim a missional imagination as a faith leader. Divided into three sections: "Daily Readings on Missional Engagement Like Jesus," "Daily Readings on Ministry Development Like Jesus," and "Daily Readings on Leadership Effectiveness Like Jesus," the sixty short reflections are framed biblically, offer real-life stories, and invite leaders to meditate on their own ministry and setting. The reflections invite readers into deeper reflection on what it means to be more like Jesus in all they do, think, and believe. Work-ing through one reflection a day would ground the reader's ministry in a pat-tern of action/reflection/action that could well be repeated after sixty days. As with reading the same biblical story over and over, planters will likely gain new insights with each experience and thus continue to become more like Jesus.

—**Betsy Miller**, President,
Moravian Church Northern Province

It is vital that church planters be deeply rooted in the Word of God. As a wise, experienced church planting leader, Ben provides a helpful resource to help church planters abide in Christ as their first and most important task. I plan to provide a copy for each of our planters!

—**Amy R. Schenkel**, Great Lakes Regional
Mission Leader, Resonate Global Mission

Each thoughtful, empathetic insight invites the planter to take the next step, crest the hill, turn the corner, and keep on keeping on in helping people grow in their relationship with God. Great encouragement for spiritual entrepreneurs!

—**Dr. George Johnson**, Executive Director,
Christian Evangelistic Association

Ben has created a biblically rooted guide for church planters that is helpful in both hearing the scriptures and applying that wisdom to the everyday challenges of planting. As such, Ben's work is a useful guide to keep planters rooted in God and moving forward in their calling. I highly recommend it.

—**Rev. Larry Doornbos**, Director of Vibrant Congregations,
Reformed Church in America/
Christian Reformed Church in North America

Ben Ingebretson understands church planting and church planters. *Plant Like Jesus* is a valuable resource for helping planters stay connected to Jesus through the different stages of starting a church. The practical and insightful studies will allow a planter to navigate the planting journey while refueling spiritually. This will be a required resource for our church planters.

—**Lance Hurley**, Executive Director,
Ignite Church Planting: Chicagoland

The vast majority of church planting resources are loaded with great information about research-based best practices, strategies, and techniques for planting effective churches. *Plant Like Jesus* redirects planters back to the One who is building his church, encouraging them to calibrate their efforts to his ways and purposes, providing an essential foundation every emerging church deeply needs. I highly recommend this critical resource.

—**Steve Pike**, President, Urban Islands Project

What a gift this collection is for pioneers navigating leadership and disciple making in the Fresh Expressions movement of church. It inspires and encourages the soul while hitting on all of the important aspects of contextual church planting.

—**Heather Evans**, Pastor of Fresh Expressions
at Grace Church, Cape Coral, Florida

These devotions bring together rich biblical reflection and hard-won wisdom from the field in helping church planters ground their work in God's reconciliation of the world in Christ. They will inspire, enrich, and refocus anyone called to this vital ministry.

—**Dwight Zscheile**, Vice President of Innovation and
Associate Professor of Congregational Mission and Leadership,
Luther Seminary, St. Paul, Minnesota

One of the most neglected areas in church planting can be a planter's own spiritual life. It's easy to become so consumed in the preparation for launching a church that a planter can feel lost in the shuffle. Ingebretson's *Plant Like Jesus* is a practical guide to resource planters or any spiritual entrepreneur in their spiritual journey.

—**Rev. Dr. Rosario "Roz" Picardo**, Dean of the Chapel and Director of the Pohly Center for Supervision and Leadership Formation, United Theological Seminary and Co-Pastor of Mosaic Church

Ben brings decades of potent church planting wisdom to every page of *Plant Like Jesus*. But since his primary source is the revelation of Jesus in scripture as our model for ministry, this book is timeless and relevant in ways only possible coming from Jesus directly, the Lord of the church of all times and all places and all peoples. This book is a gift to the church! I can't wait to get my hands on many copies. Every church planter will be edified by the best practices of the world's best leader, Jesus. His ways are higher than our ways, and the wise listen and learn. Jesus is the most servant-hearted, empowering, and sacrificial leader ever. We will need the help of the same Holy Spirit filling us to walk in his footprints.

—**Tim Vink**, Senior Catalyst for Church Multiplication, Reformed Church in America

Someone has said that church planting is the extreme sport in ministry. As a church planter myself, I agree with that statement. My friend Ben Ingebretson has written a great resource to help church planters remain grounded in the remarkable practices of Jesus while focusing on their important work. *Plant Like Jesus* is a collection of sixty brief devotions that are biblical and practical. The strength of the book derives from the fact that Ben is a reflective practitioner; he has planted churches, has led church planting movements, and has been training church planters across North America for many years. He well understands the need for church planters to always feed their souls as Jesus did during his earthly ministry.

— **Rev. Eddy Alemán**, General Secretary, Reformed Church in America

This helpful resource not only nourishes the soul of the planter but also helps the church planter and planting teams to think biblically about their work. I am recommending it to the planters in our network.

—**Jim Lankheet**, Executive Director and President, Coram Deo Association of Churches

Effective church planters seek to engage with God as they apply biblical principles in their ministry context. *Plant Like Jesus* provides soulful and strategic insights to encourage the heart and to guide the new church developer in the planting process. I recommend this valuable resource.

—**Dr. Robert E. Logan**, author of
The Church Planting Journey and *The Discipleship Difference*

In *Plant Like Jesus*, Rev. Ben Ingebretson paints a gallery of biblical, theological, and practical portraits where the reader can stroll, ponder, and envision living out Jesus' example for us. Each daily reading invites the reader to walk with Jesus and follow his missional and organizational model for starting faith communities. Read this book and be encouraged; you are the one missing from this divine work of art!

—**Rev. Eliseo A. Mejia-Leiva**
Fresh Expressions Director and Pastor,
First Paris United Methodist Church

Church planting can be described as being similar to deep space exploration, exploring the Sahara, or a solo trip to Antarctica. The work done by church planters can leave even the strongest leaders feeling isolated and overwhelmed. In *Plant Like Jesus*, Reverend Ingebretson encourages you to stay connected with the true inspiration, wisdom, and hope found in Jesus. He provides practical ways to reconnect with Jesus, providing a foundation as you journey through the realm of planting something original. This must-read book is for planters wanting to connect with Jesus on a new level. As you read about the examples of planters, you will be able to apply their successes and challenges in your own ministry. This encouraging devotional book targets the heart of the planter, providing a Pauline concept to ministry. Ingebretson's wisdom and experience gives him front-row knowledge of what makes church plants successful churches. The crisp devotionals are a reminder that God is working in all things, both our successes and our growth areas as planters. Stay connected, create your rhythm, and allow God to work through you and all those that have come before.

—**Jason Mehring**
Church Planter
Fargo, North Dakota

Amidst all the tools outlining the best practices, models, and strategies of church planting, one essential resource has been missing. *Plant Like Jesus* fills that gap with daily reminders of the divine wisdom, direction, and power that has already been provided to us by Jesus, the head of the church.

—**Dr. Randy Weener**
Director of Church Multiplication,
Reformed Church in America

While there are church planting works based on modern-day theories, strategies, and philosophies, *Plant Like Jesus* is a unique creation, a delight, emerging from the author's own passion and incredible experience. This book is a must-read for church planters to stay grounded in scripture and in Jesus' vision for the church.

—**Rev. Dr. Jebasingh Jebamony**
Planter, Multicultural Community Church

Ben Ingebretson brings years of experience as a church planter and a leader of church planters to this book. From this, he candidly acknowledges the myriad experiences church planters face, reminding planters that there is grace, guidance, and peace for them in the life, teachings, and ministry of Jesus Christ.

—**Mark Teasdale**
Garrett Evangelical Theological Seminary, Chicago, Illinois

In church planting, a common mistake is to focus too much on strategy and technique and not enough on the spiritual readiness of the leaders called to the task. This book is for you and your leaders. While you are developing budgets, creating those fancy websites, and organizing events, read this book so that you can prepare your hearts.

—**Matt Miofsky**, Pastor of The Gathering and
author of *Let Go: Leaning into the Future Without Fear*

In all the flurry of church-planting activity—trainings, conferences, books, seminars, webinars, thought leaders, strategies, assessments—have we ever stopped and asked the question, "How could we plant a church like Jesus?" That is at the heart of *Plant Like Jesus*—emulating and following Jesus as we seek to birth new communities of more Jesus followers.

—**Dr. Sean Benesh**, author of
The Adventure of Vocation, director of Intrepid, and
Senior Editor of the International Journal of Urban Transformation

Over the years, I have participated in many dozens of church planter assessments, both formally and informally. One of the most difficult traits to discern in these is the dimension of wisdom. The approach Ingebretson takes in *Plant Like Jesus* is bound to help move planters in the direction of real personal growth in this area. He offers a sound, biblical perspective in his series of readings, plus exercises that stimulate both reflection and application. Really helpful, challenging, and necessary!

—**Dr. Linda Bergquist**
Church Planting Catalyst, North American Mission Board

Plant Like Jesus will be an essential resource for planters and agents of change as these leaders move forward in the lonely and challenging terrain of church planting.

—**Brad Aycock,** Director,
New Church Development, West Ohio Conference

PLANT

LIKE

JESUS

THE CHURCH PLANTER'S DEVOTIONAL

BEN INGEBRETSON

UPPER ROOM BOOKS®
NASHVILLE

Library of Congress Cataloging-in-Publication Data

Names: Ingebretson, Ben, 1957- author.
Title: Plant like Jesus : the church planter's devotional / Ben Ingebretson.
Description: Nashville, TN : Upper Room Books, 2021. | Includes bibliographical references. | Summary: "Plant Like Jesus is food for the soul for spiritual pioneers, church planters, and those seeking to start a new worship service or worship site. Sixty concise readings draw readers back into the practices of Jesus, who taught essential lessons for church planters. Readings are organized around three categories: missional engagement, ministry development, and effective leadership. Plant Like Jesus sources the best of best practices of Jesus himself and the early Christian movement. Readings include scriptural reference, biblical and theological reflection, practical field illustrations, a directed meditation, and prayer. Plant Like Jesus is daily spiritual fuel for mission work today. It is ideal for planting leaders, multiplying congregations, innovating pastors, restart leaders, and anyone seeking to anchor their work in the practices of Jesus"-- Provided by publisher.
Identifiers: LCCN 2020034281 (print) | LCCN 2020034282 (ebook) | ISBN 9780835819473 (paperback) | ISBN 9780835819480 (mobi) | ISBN 9780835819497 (epub)
Subjects: LCSH: Church development, New--Prayers and devotions. | Jesus Christ--Example--Prayers and devotions.
Classification: LCC BV652.24 .I545 2021 (print) | LCC BV652.24 (ebook) | DDC 254/.1--dc23
LC record available at https://lccn.loc.gov/2020034281
LC ebook record available at https://lccn.loc.gov/2020034282

Print ISBN: 978-0-8358-1947-3
Mobi ISBN: 978-0-8358-1948-0
Epub ISBN: 978-0-8358-1949-7

Printed in the United States of America

To all those who dream of new kingdom adventures
that are deeply rooted in Jesus

CONTENTS

Part 1
DAILY READINGS ON MISSIONAL ENGAGEMENT LIKE JESUS

Part 2
DAILY READINGS ON ORGANIZATIONAL DEVELOPMENT LIKE JESUS

Part 3
DAILY READINGS ON LEADERSHIP EFFECTIVENESS LIKE JESUS

FOREWORD

Church planting is hard work. I know that from personal experience. When I started Embrace Church fourteen years ago, we called ourselves "The New Church" for the first few months because our church didn't have a name and we had only thirty-some people. We didn't get to be the church we are today overnight (or even over hundreds of nights!), and there were a lot of times when I wanted to give up on everything and just quit.

I'm glad I didn't.

Plant Like Jesus is a book I wish twenty-four-year-old Adam Weber would have had when he started this whole church-planting adventure. Not because Ben's words would have helped me do anything different strategy-wise, but more so because twenty-four-year-old Adam (and thirty-eight-year-old Adam too!) desperately needed that simple-yet-powerful foundation of Jesus guiding my every action, plan, and dream for what my church was then and would later become. I've known Ben, now, for quite a few years, and I don't think there's anyone more qualified to write this book than him. Like the apostle Paul, Ben bridges that gap between the two worlds church planters all too often feel pulled between: telling new people about Jesus and coming up with all the strategy and best practices behind that greater goal.

As Paul did with the early church, Ben bridges that gap through each of his meditations on the different elements of church planting found throughout this book. Breaking things up into sections—meditations on missional engagement, meditations on organizational development, and meditations on effective leadership—Ben easily transitions between more-spiritual reflections and words that are just plain practical. ("There's a chapter on organizational restructuring, 'System Tune-up'? Gold.")

There's a lot of noise out there when it comes to church planting. Much like a lot of things these days, opinions, strategies, and those who want to see you fail are everywhere. My advice? If you're a church planter, delete Instagram . . . and Facebook . . . and maybe throw away your phone! I'm kidding, but Ben is spot-on when he writes that the goal of planting a church is filled with a lot of challenges, and those challenges don't stop at decisions about worship service times, whether to rent or buy a building, and how to manage staff.

Being a church planter can be—scratch that, *will* be—mentally, spiritually, and emotionally exhausting. "Easy" wasn't what we signed up for when we agreed to plant a church, but that doesn't mean we need to burn ourselves out in the process. *Plant Like Jesus* is one of many much-needed resources, whether this is your first or fifteenth time planting a church. Because ultimately, planting a church begins and ends with Jesus. Period. And that's exactly what Ben's book is about.

Sure, there are a lot of practical tips and tricks in the following pages, but you can get tips and tricks from Google. What Ben offers here is as much *spiritual practice* as it is *how-to guide*. I'm no longer in the day-to-day messiness of church planting (thank you, Jesus!), but Ben's meditations on community engagement, resilience, and comparison are no less relevant to my job as a pastor now than they were ten years ago. They might even be more applicable now, as I wrestle not with how to get more people through the door on a Sunday morning but how to keep them there, engaged and growing in their walk with Jesus.

I hope you enjoy the words in this book as much as I did. They're not always easy words to swallow, easy words to pray, or easy words to put into practice; but, again, that's kind of the point. Jesus didn't give you an easy job when he called you to plant a church; he gave you a necessary, joy-filled, rewarding, and kingdom-impacting kind of job. What you do with the people, the church you've been entrusted with, is vitally important, and Ben doesn't sugarcoat that here. What he does do, is give us practical tools, wise words, and powerful prayers to reach that next person for Jesus.

I hope you will read what he has to say. Take it in. Then go out and do what you were called to do: Plant like Jesus.

—Adam Weber
Embrace Church

ACKNOWLEDGMENTS

The seeds of *Plant Like Jesus* were first sown into the soil of my life in 1985, when I was sent out to plant a church not having been assessed, trained, or coached. That experience profoundly humbled me, as I stumbled forward, an inexperienced planting pioneer. How could I ever forget the years of contract painting work (climbing forty-foot ladders to paint Michigan barns) and the struggle to balance ministry and marketplace as a bivocational planter? I am most grateful to God, who redeemed all of that frustration more than I ever could have imagined through the opportunity to serve dozens of church planters as a friend, coach, and supervisor since 2002.

I am grateful for the Reformed Church in America, particularly Tim Vink and Sherwin Weener, along with dozens of planters and planting teams who worked with me during the season of "Our Call" to plant a new wave of gospel-centered churches. This book draws upon those years.

I am also grateful for the Dakotas and Minnesota United Methodist Church, Bishop Bruce Ough, and planters who welcomed me and gave me the remarkable opportunity to return to my midwestern home turf and lead planting efforts there. This book also draws upon those efforts as well.

All of the field stories cited arise from actual planting cases. In some of the stories, I have changed names and location details so as to preserve the confidentiality of those involved.

Finally, I am grateful to my parents, who pointed me toward the mission of God; and my wonderful wife, Karen, who supports me in this work with all of its travels, sharing with me a concern for the new churches.

Soli Deo Gloria.

Introduction

WHY THIS BOOK AND HOW TO USE IT

Read John 15:4; I Corinthians 3:5-14.

> *"Remain in me, as I also remain in you. No branch can bear fruit by itself; it must remain in the vine. Neither can you bear fruit unless you remain in me."*
>
> —John 15:4

Sometimes, church planting can make you feel as if you are living in two utterly different worlds.

One world is characterized by a call from God to risk much in a venture of faith. It is about a vision for a new Jesus community that is authentic, winsome, and innovative. We imagine pouring new wine into new wineskins and engaging people in the radical life of Jesus.

A light year away is the other world, characterized by metrics and methods tied to strategies and best practices. This world can be like pouring flat soda into a paper cup. Of course, this technical side of church planting is needed; we know that. But if only we could see how these two worlds can connect; if only we could abide in the life-giving vine in the day-to-day myriad tasks planters do (see John 15:4). If only we could source our best practices back to the way of Jesus himself.

In 1 Corinthians 3, the apostle Paul points us to a bridge between the two worlds into which planters can feel pulled. He did his fair share of pioneer planting work, by some estimations starting more than fourteen churches. Paul, along with Apollos, planted the church in Corinth. In his mind, Paul had to do his part; but in the end, it was God who made the church grow.

There is good news for us in that little explanation: Paul did not carry the weight of success on his shoulders, for he saw a connection between his practices and a spiritual dynamic. Look closely at how Paul describes that connection: "By the grace of God I laid a foundation as a wise builder" (1 Cor. 3:10). Here, Paul identifies a wisdom that is essential in planting work, and that wisdom has to do with the foundation. Paul changes the metaphor from "planting" to "building" to call out the importance of getting the early work—the foundational work—done the right way. And for Paul, the right way to go about this is clear: "For no one can lay any foundation other than the one that has been laid; that foundation is Jesus Christ" (1 Cor. 3:11, NRSV). In other words, the right way to start a church is the Jesus way. Obvious? Maybe or maybe not.

Here is the deal: As a start-up leader, it is easy to drift into a "worlds-apart" gap between our message ("Jesus is Lord") and our methods (a hodge-podge of strategies we pick up from seminars and books). Paul advises that we close that gap. He teaches that the good message of the gospel also has a good *method*, whereby it roots a community. *Plant Like Jesus* is an effort to close the gap by tracing a taproot of planting wisdom deep into the teachings and example of Jesus. The meditations in this book are clustered in three categories: "Missional Engagement," "Organizational Development," and "Leadership Effectiveness." This wisdom from Jesus, according to Paul, is the key to our start-up work standing the test of time (see 1 Corinthians 3:12-14).

Here is a way to rise above all the noise that can surround start-up work. We must begin with Jesus. Christology teaches us how we do missiology and ecclesiology. Jesus teaches us how to engage people in culture, forming new disciples and leading to a new community of faith. We can truly go to our Lord to guide us in demonstrating and declaring the kingdom, raising up leaders, forming teams, and communicating in order to connect powerfully with new people. Jesus can teach us about fundraising, dealing with setbacks, casting vision, and so much more. Jesus, and the way the early church followed his example, gives us a pathway to follow. He is not only the Lord of the church but also the Lord of church planting. This is good news.

The fact that you have read this far suggests you are at least a little curious about what it might mean to go back to Jesus for the methods in your ministry. So, how might you follow that curious impulse and go deeper into both the story of Jesus and the story of the new church you are developing, with an eye toward integrating the two? How can your work be both effective and more deeply spiritual as the Lord of the church leads you? I believe the sixty meditations contained in this book can help, and you could use them in the following ways.

- Use them as devotionals to anchor your daily time for personal meditation and reflection for sixty days. Take perhaps thirty minutes of quiet sometime during the day to orient your agenda to the Lord's. Use the prayers and reflection questions purposefully for deep integration.
- If you are married, invite your spouse to join you in the reading so your partner can appreciate the deep work of spiritual integration and reflection you are embarking upon. Let this be a place where you meet for prayers and meditation around the busy and often frenetic planting work that can consume your household.
- Consider the sixty devotionals as a two-months-long deep dive into planter training with Jesus. Invite your key leaders and coach to read along with you, scheduling time for group reflection and discussion. Roll out your planning documents and ask where the principles of Jesus need to impact your design and field work together.
- Return to *Plant Like Jesus* annually as a spiritual retreat. Take two months a year using the sixty readings in your daily devotional time and your annual planting "checkup." Note how the Spirit prompts you in each reading, and journal your thoughts in the margins of the book so that each year you can reflect upon your progress and growth.

Your curiosity to plant a church like Jesus would is a spiritual hunger that I believe Jesus will satisfy, if you pursue it. After all, he said, "Search, and you will find" (Matt. 7:7, NRSV). I hope that your search in these pages will lead you to finding Jesus alive, full of wisdom and inviting you to follow him in your ministry adventure!

Part 1

Daily Readings on
Missional Engagement Like Jesus

1

SETTLING INTO A PLACE

Read John 1:1-14.

> *The Word became flesh and made his dwelling among us.*
> *We have seen his glory, the glory of the one and only Son,*
> *who came from the Father, full of grace and truth.*
>
> —John 1:14

How "settled in" are you? Before much else happened in our Lord's ministry, he settled in. It is a profound reality, when you think about it.

Consider how the Incarnation did not take place apart from settling in and settling down into a street address and ZIP code. Jesus could have taken up humanness without taking up a specific human place, and we still would have the mystery of the Incarnation to proclaim at Christmas. But Jesus took the work of incarnation a second step, when he settled into a particular geography, a specific people, and a specific town.

So, what was "settling in" like for Jesus? Let's start with family and his relatives. We know Jesus had family and that his family experience was not always smooth (see Mark 6:3; John 7:5). The fact that Jesus remained in Nazareth for many of his early years means that it was likely Jesus settled into those family relationships. Imagine the house of Joseph and its summer reunion picnic. Picture the Jesus who turned the world upside down in a few short, final years, unhurried on relaxed weekends with family and friends during his early years.

Consider again the settled experience of thirty years spent in Nazareth—all that time Jesus spent in the common village spaces and connecting with people in their homes. It must have been a somewhat unremarkable time, as little has come down to us in teaching or miracles from those years. During that season, we know Jesus' parents took him to the Temple every year (see Luke 2:41 and following), and he likely had his bar mitzvah at age thirteen. We know he was a carpenter (see Mark 6:3) and that he likely worked alongside Joseph contracting with local households in his trade. Picture Jesus bartering his skills for pay or food or rent. Imagine those negotiations and then Jesus delivering a finished product. Imagine Jesus building trust with clients to maintain and grow a business. Picture Jesus gradually settling into a network of business connections.

Now, we know that when Jesus "moved into the neighborhood" (John 1:14, The Message), he did not stay put in Nazareth. But he did remain within that rather small cultural and geographical vicinity. The region of Galilee, an area roughly the size of the state of Rhode Island, confined the Lord of the universe for much of his early work. There, Jesus built a ministry of healing and teaching. He did that relationship upon relationship, experience upon experience, layer upon layer, year upon year. He settled into Galilee, and he gave that process considerable time. Picture Jesus, rising most days not in a hurry to save the world, but making his way, one step at a time, to his home-improvement clients around Nazareth.

Church planters take their cue from the Incarnation not only as a principle of making the gospel relevant and practical in real-life ways but also in settling down into the life of a particular place; moving from being an outsider to being an insider; starting as a joiner rather than as a leader. Building trust one experience, one relationship, one day at a time, layer upon layer. Jeremy is a friend and planter who discovered how important it is to settle into local community networks. Joining Business Network International (BNI) became an avenue for him to demonstrate that practice. BNI has thousands of networks worldwide that exist to promote local community referrals, all based upon relationships. It's an affiliation not unlike Rotary or Kiwanis. Members rotate and are given the opportunity to share their work, and they thereby gain referrals through trusted relationships. Jeremy's participation in BNI speaks volumes to others about his desire to settle in. It moves Jeremy into the neighborhood.

It is the nature of our hyper-communication culture for us often to see others' success as coming quickly. Those stories travel, and it is tempting to feel envious. But the first message that comes from Jesus is to settle in. This means putting aside our regimented schedules and plans (as though we could map all this out and "do" rather than first "be"). First, we make a commitment to know *this* place and *these* people—to be fully present in this place. Settling is the first step in planting like Jesus.

Reflect: Meditate upon John 1:14. To what extent are you at peace with the incarnational work of settling into your community? What actions would send the signal to yourself and others that you are committing to know and love this place and these people long term? What difference will it make for you and your family to settle into your community for the long haul?

Prayer: *God of heaven and earth, thank you for the example of Jesus, who deeply committed to a people and a place. I recognize that I feel the urge to hurry things that cannot be hurried. Teach me the settled way of Jesus, who was fully present where he was. Amen.*

⊰ 2 ⊱

FIRST, LISTEN

Read Mark 10:46-52; Luke 24:17-19.

> *[Jesus] asked them, "What are you discussing together as you walk along?" They stood still, their faces downcast. One of them, named Cleopas, asked him, "Are you the only one visiting Jerusalem who does not know the things that have happened there in these days?" "What things?" he asked.*
>
> —Luke 24:17-19

You are answering a question that no one is asking." That blunt statement stopped me cold in my tracks. When I was able to get past my annoyed confusion and actually hear what was being said, I felt embarrassed, and I relearned an important lesson. To quote Bono of U2, "It's hard to listen while you preach."[1] To quote Proverbs, "To answer before listening—that is folly and shame" (Prov. 18:13). We cannot overstate the importance of listening for spiritual pioneers, particularly when we observe the practice of Jesus himself.

It can be tempting to think that when Jesus was present, he filled up a room with his words; perhaps you know of someone who does just that. We can get the idea that Jesus showed up, and immediately he began to teach and preach as is recorded in the Gospels, with the Sermon on the Mount or some of his many parables. However, if you consider the number of words we actually have from Jesus and the number of years he actively ministered, it is likely that he listened far more than he spoke. For example, in Mark 10, he hears Bartimaeus through the clamor of a crowd and his cry for help, "Jesus, Son of David, have mercy on me!" (v. 47). Here, Jesus shows us his ability to tune out the noise around him so he can hear what is essential, a cry for mercy.

Planters can do no less when distracting noise fills the air and we need to hear the nearly silent cry of our community. So often, listening is the key to unlocking profound understanding. Rick Warren was deeply listening and heard the local plea when he was planting Saddleback Church in Southern California. Imagine the distracting noise he was up against in a community where so many people were preoccupied with the pursuit of success and happiness. When *The Purpose Driven Life* was released with the subtitle *What on Earth Am I Here For?* Rick touched a sensitive nerve. He also showed that he had been listening like Jesus, who heard the cry of Bartimaeus. Listening to the wider community to hear their collective yearning unlocked a remarkable planting opportunity for Rick, and the rest, as they say, is history. As my mother used to tell me, "You have two ears and only one mouth." This truth still applies.

Further examples of Jesus' practice of listening are so common in the Gospels that we might pass right over them. When Jesus posed a powerful question, he opened space and attention for a reply. Our Lord was fond of using questions to prompt a conversation, and these questions were not always rhetorical; he genuinely wanted to hear and contemplate an answer.

In Luke 24, Jesus does just this with his disciples along the Emmaus road. Here, Jesus shows us how to listen deeply. Notice how he does not barge in and quickly answer all the disciples' questions with a long narrative but rather keeps probing their hearts and minds so he can listen to them: "What are you discussing together as you walk along?" (v. 17). And then, after they provide a very short reply, he goes further, asking, "What things?" so as to draw out their deepest thoughts. Jesus wants to hear them out.

One of the bad habits we can fall into is to fill up the silence with our words just about the time someone is trying to tell us what they are truly feeling or thinking. Filling up silence with our words is often about our commitment to our assumptions and our own agenda. Jesus, by contrast, is often genuinely curious to hear the other person.

Observing, noticing, listening: These practices can keep us from making false assumptions about people and about our mission field. Our ears can keep us from answering questions no one is really asking, so that we can get to the ones they *are* asking. Listening also wins us favor with folks who generally appreciate it when we take a heartfelt interest in them. Little wonder that Jesus drew others into his mission: They felt *heard*.

Immanuel, "God with us," was more than a bumper-sticker slogan in Galilee. People experienced a deep connection with Jesus because he listened.

Reflect: How would those around you describe your listening skills? What have you heard to be the heart-cry of your community? How often do you listen deeply to someone?

Prayer: *Teach me, Lord Jesus, to listen as you did. Help me to be slow to speak, slow to judge, and quick to hear. Open my ears so that I can sense both the cry for help around me and your Spirit more clearly, that I might follow you more completely. I pray, in Jesus' name. Amen.*

❈ 3 ❈

COMMUNITY ENGAGEMENT

Read Matthew 4:23-25.

> *[Jesus] said, "I must proclaim the good news of the kingdom*
> *of God to the other towns also, because that is why I was*
> *sent."*
>
> —Luke 4:43

By far, the message and word that most characterized the ministry of Jesus pertained to the *kingdom*. The word appears 162 times in the New Testament.[1] *Kingdom* signals the rule of Jesus (see Luke 1:33), the rightful rule and reign of God in the world (see Matthew 6:10).

The church has a very specific role in expanding the kingdom. However, the kingdom and the church are not identical. The church points toward and leads into the fullness of God's kingdom reign when all of creation is put back right as God intended from the beginning. It has a "now and not yet" reality, as we see signs of the lordship of Jesus in our world while we anticipate the full recovery of what was lost in the rebellion brought on by sin. Peter says it this way: "In keeping with his promise we are looking forward to a new heaven and a new earth, where righteousness dwells" (2 Pet. 3:13).

Look closely at how Jesus demonstrates and declares the kingdom in the gospel records: "Jesus went throughout Galilee, teaching in their synagogues and proclaiming the good news of the kingdom and curing every disease and every sickness among the people" (Matthew 4:23, NRSV). The rule of God has come in the mission of Jesus. It is not just a vague agenda to put a patch on things but a radical invasion of heaven in the person of Christ (see Luke 17:21). Proclaiming the reign of God immediately puts us in mission to an imperfect, broken world loved by God. Jesus began that effort as he healed the sick and liberated those who were in spiritual bondage. While his teaching drew great crowds later, the early crowds came for healing. The initial "buzz" that was felt across Galilee, Jerusalem, Judea, and the regions of Jordan and that elicited a response was the healing work of Jesus as he deeply identified with people in their physical predicament.

Matthew and Mark interestingly include the Decapolis in the list of places where Jesus drew a crowd of early followers as he demonstrated the kingdom in healing. The Decapolis was a collection of ten cities that were distinctly Greco-Roman, not Jewish, in their culture. As Jesus declared the kingdom, he reached beyond his tribe into a diverse world hungry for hope and healing. He connected with a wide range of people in their struggle.

Jesus teaches us that early in our work we are wise to seek out those areas in the community where healing and hope are desperately needed and then serve those needs. The Jesus way is to call attention to the reign of God by responding to specific concerns. Recently, I heard a story of a planter who did this by surveying dozens of community leaders (or more), and he discovered that the local elementary school was struggling. So, together, they organized a benefit to raise funds to repair a playground, followed by multiple efforts to bless the teachers, students, and families with school supplies. That organizing and benefiting engaged many community people who had no affiliation with a church. Relationships were built, and that struggling school experienced a kingdom blessing. A new church engaged the community in a helpful way, and there was a bit of a community buzz from that activity. Those relationships and that rapport became significant as the ministry unfolded.

Oftentimes, we are not alone in hearing a local cry for help, and we are wise to collaborate in our reply. One local spiritual pioneer, hearing the pain of divorce in their community, gathered local leaders from the fields of mental health, education, health care, and representative faith groups to address marital health issues in a proactive way. Together, they formed a collective rotating premarital education series for couples. The whole effort knit together dozens of new partnerships, and the entire community benefited as more couples entered marriage better prepared for the journey. Another planter partnered her start-up group with Habitat for Humanity to build a home for a family prior to starting any worship and in that practice set a deep kingdom value into the plant identity.

Early on in his ministry, Jesus paced himself to the needs of his community. He connected deeply with their predicament before he fully developed his teaching ministry and in doing so shows us the priority of effective community service and engagement.

Reflect: You are called to announce the kingdom, the rightful rule of God, in the very community you are serving. What does that look like for you? With whom might you need to connect to discover needs that could raise the hopes of many people, as Jesus did? How can you create a buzz of service and healing in your community early in your work?

Prayer: *Healing Jesus, this community needs the hope of the kingdom. Help me discover the deep needs in this place and to feel the deep predicament of people. Show me partners who might lead to a powerful expression of your kingdom. Bring this community your hope, I pray. Amen.*

❖ 4 ❖

FIRST FOLLOWERS

Read John 1:35-50.

> *As Jesus was walking beside the Sea of Galilee, he saw two brothers, Simon called Peter and his brother Andrew. They were casting a net into the lake, for they were fishermen. "Come, follow me," Jesus said, "and I will send you out to fish for people." At once they left their nets and followed him.*
>
> —Matthew 4:18-20

Sociologists at the Pew Research Center who study religion in America report that Americans are a mix of non-practicing Christian, practicing Christian, atheist, agnostic, and other faiths.[1] Religious practice in America is a dynamic and changing landscape that can make for some fascinating reading and attention-getting trends. Immigration, generational preferences, and the rise of "none-and-dones" are just a few of the factors that significantly impact trends. With such a complex mix of religious practices, where do you start in forming a new Christian community? Once again, our eyes turn to Jesus, who also faced a culture with mixed religious practices and preferences.

While Jesus likely knew well the various religious movements and traditions of his time, including those of Judaism and Greco-Roman paganism, he saw individuals and seemed to begin at that level. There would be no great public ministry before he had developed particular people, one at a time. He did not seem to be in a big rush to identify the Twelve; he was intentional, deliberate. Our text today describes how Jesus called individuals, beginning with Andrew, Peter, Philip, and Nathaniel. James, the brother of John, does not join the group until some months later (see Mark 1:19). Matthew (or Levi, as he was also known) comes into the group on another occasion, when Jesus is passing through Capernaum (see Mark 2:13-14). Jesus seems to be looking for someone as he forms his band, but not just anyone.

That discerning eye saw some qualities that are worth considering. None of the disciples had religious credentials or Levitical pedigree. In fact, most of them had no claim to being educated but instead were considered "uneducated and ordinary" (Acts 4:13, NRSV). Nor were any particularly wealthy, as most of them came from rural Galilee. But what Jesus did seem to see was their desire for an authentic encounter with God. That was key. Some were connected with John the Baptist and his reforms (see John 1:35). They all likely were well aware of religiosity around them, but those routines left them wanting more.

Jesus may have seen in this eclectic group of persons a representation of many others he would attract later. Maybe he saw them as networked to others with a similar hunger. Most important, Jesus saw their desire to engage and be formed by him. That quality of curiosity and readiness to spend time with Jesus was essential, and so their adventure began: "What are you looking for? . . . Come and see" (vv. 38-39, NRSV).

Veteran planters know how critical those first joiners are. They know that those individuals will network us either to lots of other churchy folks or to people more likely to be spiritually curious. Those first followers can connect us into a world of family systems, workplace networks, neighborhood associations, or social media contacts. One of those networks, the family system or *Oikos* ("household"), is cited throughout the Gospels and the book of Acts as being integral to advancing the mission (see Mark 5:19; Luke 19:9; John 4:53). We are wise to follow Jesus closely when we make choices about who we invest our time in from the start. Are they hungry for something more? Are they dissatisfied with status quo religion? Are they ready to engage the kingdom firsthand with doubts and tentative-yet-significant new steps of faith? Are they ready to explore the real deal?

Rachel tells about the first followers at her plant being self-described "spiritual nomads." They had a hunger for God but had never found a place to live that out. This ragtag group of teachers, military people, and other professionals had a vision for how church could transform their community, although they had little experience of church within their backgrounds. It was a vision that may never have taken hold quite the same if the early adopters primarily had been churchy people looking for another churchy experience.

The pressure to develop a launching team is most always present in church planting. "Warm bodies" are never turned away when it comes to public worship. But when it comes to recruiting our first followers—our early adopters—Jesus shows us wise discernment.

Reflect: How does the example of Jesus help you think about your choices regarding in whom you will invest time? How can you discern potential followers' hunger for an authentic walk with Jesus? What will you do to give them a taste of a discipleship journey?

Prayer: *Jesus, I never want to lose my hunger for an authentic experience with you. As I seek to develop disciples, I too seek after you. I want to be shaped by you and your Spirit. Lead me to those who desire an authentic experience with you and your kingdom. Amen.*

⁘ 5 ⁘

LIMINAL SPACES

Read Luke 10:1-9; Acts 16:13-15.

> *"When you enter a house, first say, 'Peace to this house.' If someone who promotes peace is there, your peace will rest on them; if not, it will return to you. Stay there, eating and drinking whatever they give you."*
>
> —Luke 10:5-7

The word *liminal* means "threshold." Liminal places are transition places. Life is full of liminal spaces. For example, every real estate sign represents at least two families passing through a transition. Who among us has not navigated that crazy space of loading up, unloading, and then making sense of new schools, new traffic patterns, new relationships, and a new schedule for the trash pickup? Transitions take place when people step into an uncharted phase of life, such as a job transfer, marriage, parenthood, retirement, or career change. Some transitions are particularly painful, such as divorce, loss of a job, or even sending your last child off to college. Jesus likely pointed toward liminal spaces when he sent out his disciples. He knew how people in transition are spiritually open in ways others may not be.

In Luke 10, the writer reveals how relationships can unfold in a powerful kingdom direction when we discover someone at a threshold. As the story plays out, Jesus sends seventy-two disciples ahead of him to the towns and places he intends to go, taking little with them other than a prayer and an eye for an open home. The name that is often given to this hospitable individual who may receive them is "person of peace." Finding such a person of peace is to discover an individual who is spiritually open. Paul was following this practice of Jesus when he and Silas connected with Lydia in Philippi and stayed at her home (see Acts 16:13-15). Philippi was a Gentile community and a key Roman trade center. The fact that Lydia was a "worshiper of God" (v. 14) indicates that she fell into a class of Gentiles who were interested in an authentic encounter with God. She was what we might call "spiritual but not religious." Both Jesus and Paul recognized that liminal spaces can position people in a new potential relationship to the kingdom.

We tend to lose sight of how significant transitions are if we have not experienced one recently. A job loss, a health issue, a family adjustment, a career relocation, a relational struggle, or just a new phase of life can throw lots of confusion and questions into life. I recently spent time with a couple who were wanting to get married. One had a faith commitment, while the other did not. They both acknowledged that this new phase of their life journey would require that they both take a look at their spiritual values through fresh eyes. That conversation came after a local YMCA director (a person of peace) invited our church to provide premarital education at their facility. It was clear that God was already at work in these people, in liminal spaces, stirring up spiritual life and curiosity.

It was impossible for Paul and Silas to know they would connect with a woman in transition on the day they went to a river just outside of Philippi. The text says they began speaking with those who were gathered there for prayer, and so connected with Lydia. They may have guessed this to be a place where seekers might be found. While we understand, of course, it is important that we see people as more than just prospects for our ministry, we might imagine places today where people in transition could be found. (Think CrossFit groups, cooking classes, listings of new residents, employment services, hospitals, adult education classes, expectant parents' classes, Facebook groups, midday at coffee shops, or business meet-up groups.) We do well to seek out those places and develop relationships there.

Jesus has sent us out as he sent the seventy-two. Our sending out can feel a bit unnerving. Whom will we find "out there"? What journey are they on? What will we discover when we begin to hear their stories? What new realities are they struggling to navigate? What should we be listening for and looking for? Jesus and the early Jesus followers give us a picture of people in transition—people who, like Lydia, are looking for something more. Those experiences around personal transitions are significant, as they pry us out of our routines, out of our assumptions, and out of our preoccupations to actually consider something new.

These are ideal times for the good news of the gospel. Being attentive to people in transition is part of how we plant like Jesus.

Reflect: How alert are you to people in transition? What relationship networks might these people open up to you if you were to engage them further? What would that process look like? How are you learning to initiate and develop new relationships?

Prayer: *Lord, give me eyes for those who are "people of peace" who would be receptive to your message. Show me those who may be in transition and how their search may be a hunger for spiritual discovery. I pray for Jesus' sake. Amen.*

6

DISCIPLING NEW FOLLOWERS

Read Mark 1:14-20.

> *"The time has come," he said. "The kingdom of God has come near. Repent and believe the good news!"*
>
> —Mark 1:15

When the spiritual life awakens in a person, often there are a million questions: *Can this be so? What does this mean? Why is this as it is? There are so many questions I want to ask!* Walking with someone in a new spiritual journey is a hike through a maze of curiosities and thoughts that are being tested and explored.

Jesus had a simple message for those who were spiritually awakened by his ministry. It was a message about the timeliness of his kingdom and personal transformation. Mark 1:15 is short and sweet, but as Jesus lived that message with people, the experience of a transformed life was very real. Keeping things simple is a good recipe for a discipleship movement. Look closely at what is packed into this brief prescription.

Jesus begins by telling people to take note of the time: "The time has come." Note especially, the word he uses here in Greek is the word *kairos*, which his listeners would have understood to mean "a defining moment." That reference to a special time pointed to the very ministry of Jesus, for sure; but it also pointed to the defining moment in the life of the listeners. Their life story had arrived at a defining moment. Who, hearing this provocative opener, would not lean in and want to know more? Harry Denman, the great Methodist lay evangelist, actually leveraged this principle more than any other in his work, when he would routinely ask people, "What time is it?" as a way of starting a conversation. Denman would then ask if they were aware of the defining moment this could be in their life.[1]

In the midst of a daily routine, there is an experience that catches our attention. *Whatever could be defining about this moment?* we ask ourselves. Each of us hears the answer to that question in a very personal way. Defining moments can be professional, deeply personal, relational, physical, or emotional. Imagine, for example, that a person has just received a pink slip from an employer or that they have just gotten news of a job promotion. Either way, a defining moment has arrived. Jesus further defines that moment, saying, "The kingdom of God has come near." The reign of God has entered our sphere. The kingdom is within reach of our experience. Feel the potential for a new reality greater than the present one. That job loss or job promotion is an occasion to experience the living God. Then comes the call to repent and believe. Before we impose a grim assessment of that word *repent*, let's consider the core meaning: "a change of perspective on my current dilemma." *My moment of bewilderment or struggle is replaced by the good news. God is up to something! My employment realities are known by the living God, who has purpose for me in the midst of my story.* Jesus is powerfully engaging us in these few words.

The power of this little discipleship prescription from Jesus shows up remarkably when we put it into play with a person. Imagine a young woman who struggles to make sense of her life, and she lives with a sense of futility. Your invitation to her to join a service-project team leads to a good news discovery (as her particular dilemma would have it) that she is created for a good purpose larger than herself. She is invited to change her thinking about her dilemma. Gradually, she recognizes that she is not a pointless speck in the universe but a person with purpose sent into the world to know the goodness of God and share that goodness. In time, the good news of Jesus will awaken every dimension of her life, as her journey presents other "defining moments." Of course, this conversation may take weeks or years to unfold, but it unlocks a discipleship dynamic that changes everything.

Imagine Jesus sitting with you, right now. He might ask, "What time is it for you? What is going on in your life right now? Are you aware of the good news that the kingdom is near you? Can you stretch your mind to embrace the grace, purpose, and hope I have for you?" Jesus invited people from many stations in life into his kingdom, but in each case, he tended to find the particular point of impact the kingdom brought to their dilemma. It is a good news message that radically changes everything, and it is a message central to planting like Jesus.

Reflect: How does the discipleship method of Jesus help you think about discipling your new followers? Who is God prompting you to engage with in a first-time discipleship conversation? How can you make space and time for intentional discipleship conversations?

Prayer: *Jesus, as you call me to be transformed by your grace, help me to invite others into that powerful, liberating experience. Show your timely power to transform through the good news of your kingdom, I pray. Amen.*

7

MISSIONAL IMAGINATION

Read Luke 19:1-9.

> *When Jesus reached the spot, he looked up and said to him, "Zacchaeus, come down immediately. I must stay at your house today." So he came down at once and welcomed him gladly.*

—Luke 19:5-6

Rick Richardson is the director of the Church Evangelism and Research Institutes for the Billy Graham Center at Wheaton College. Living in Chicago, he has an excellent laboratory in which to test religious assumptions and trends. Rick gives a significant part of his time and energy to exposing myths about unchurched Americans, while at the same time uncovering spiritual receptivity. What Rick exposes in his book *You Found Me: New Research on How Unchurched Nones, Millennials, and Irreligious Are Surprisingly Open to Christian Faith* is not only remarkable spiritual openness but also the tendency among church people toward doom and gloom. There is a negative narrative that is often repeated about rising secularism and religious decline that we have all heard too often.[1] Another narrative exists, however, that we should pay closer attention to. Jesus points us toward that reality in his ministry with the outsiders of his day.

In Luke 19, our Lord encounters Zacchaeus, one of the likely secular or religiously resistant people of his day. As a tax collector for Rome, he was despised for his profession, and therefore, Zacchaeus probably did not have many religious conversations with the practicing synagogue attenders in his town. Then, along comes Jesus, who sees Zacchaeus up in the tree; and the next thing you know, the two men are sharing lunch. I imagine that in so doing, Jesus gained connection to many of Zacchaeus's friends, who were similarly disconnected from organized religion yet open and curious about spirituality and faith. So there are two remarkable realities in this story: the spiritual interest of an outsider and the ability of Jesus to see and move into that reality and relationship. We can attribute the missional imagination of Jesus to his divine wisdom or to a simple bias on his part toward seeing the potential and the possible in what others quickly dismiss as impossible.

The researchers at the Pew Research Center remind us that North America today remains very spiritual, with well over half of the population believing in the power of prayer and the existence of a supreme being. It is also true that regular participation in organized religion is not the practice of most.[2] Why the disconnect? Their lives may be full; they may have felt rejected; they may have felt the church has a political agenda they cannot accept; or they may have felt the worship services they tried attending were irrelevant. Some may have felt pressured in the past and so don't feel safe in a conversation with church people. The pattern of Jesus is to move into that skeptical space (notice that Jesus does not invite Zacchaeus to his place of worship), demonstrating acceptance (see Jesus entering the house of Zacchaeus), building trust (see Jesus sharing a relaxed meal), affirming his spirituality (see Jesus affirming his new commitment to financial justice), and establishing a relational pathway for further spiritual transformation in the life of Zacchaeus and his friends. Jesus is counterintuitive: He moves toward the risky zone rather than away from it.

I admire imaginative pioneers who start faith communities in homes, on a Facebook groups platform, in laundromats, corporate offices, and, of course, pubs. Jonathan has engaged the brewhouses of Cincinnati with kingdom imagination that is indeed refreshing (in more ways than one!). Seeing the proliferation of microbreweries across his city, he recognized that these had become the spaces for networking and community life that once was the domain of religious communities. Like Jesus, Jonathan moved into that space, prompting faith conversations and pub theology groups he called Faith and Friends on Tap. In time, he was working with several brew pubs as the spiritual instigator and provocateur. In a similar fashion, Stacy launched Waffle Church for the families in her neighborhood. Saturday mornings, she got the word out through networks of kids whose parents were only too pleased to send them off for free waffles and interactive faith-forming activities. In time, the children's parents showed up, neighborhood networks were renewed, and Waffle Church became a regular Saturday event people looked forward to.

Developing that common ground allowed Jonathan and Stacy to establish a relational bridge for the good news of Jesus. It gave their new friends a place to have spiritual conversations that otherwise would never have occurred. Missional imagination is very much what is required to plant like Jesus.

Reflect: How does the missional imagination of Jesus challenge you to reconsider how you might engage people in your context? Who are those people? How might you test their receptivity? What are the next steps?

Prayer: *Jesus, you are a master at engaging people. You see the kingdom potential where I do not. Open my eyes, my ears, my heart, and my hands to follow you into new relationships, for your name's sake. Amen.*

✳ 8 ✳

IN SEARCH OF RECEPTIVITY

Read Luke 8:1-15.

After this, Jesus traveled about from one town and village to
another, proclaiming the good news of the kingdom of God.

—Luke 8:1

From time to time, I get a knock at my door from a traveling salesperson. I admire their capacity for travel amid lousy weather conditions and, above all, their ability to experience rejection. Polite as they may be, those "no-thank-you" replies must be discouraging. As a planter, I empathize.

Jesus traveled in search of receptivity. He looked for people who were ready to say "yes," and he seemed to have little time and energy for either the use of pressure tactics or pursuing those who showed disinterest. He went from town to town and from neighborhood to neighborhood in search of receptivity (see Luke 13:22). Imagine Jesus crisscrossing your community, being seen on countless street corners and engaged in coffee-shop conversations. Imagine Jesus engaging in dialogue with small-business owners, community leaders, and people walking their dogs, and him asking these people questions. Imagine those conversations. I have a hunch he would ask someone he met on the street, "Tell me about you: What do you like about living here?" "What do people around here do on the weekend?" "Who do you know who may be sick or in trouble?" "What community problems need to be solved?" Imagine the conversations—some long and some short, some people who were interested and many who were not. Imagine Jesus moving from place to place, person to person, in search of receptivity.

While the Gospel of Luke provides several pictures of Jesus in this receptivity search, it also takes us deeply into the frame of reference Jesus has as relates to that search: People are like soil. The kingdom message is like seed. Not all soils are alike. Some soil is resistant, some rocky, some thorny, and some good, and these soil types receive the seed differently. People in the business of agriculture know there is a branch of study called soil science that attempts to predict the productivity of a soil type based upon soil chemistry. Jesus is making a similar argument: Soils are different. Receptivity matters, and it cannot be controlled by the sower. For that reason, the sower must sow widely, in search of receptivity.

Some of us can drain our extroversion capacities quickly when we move from place to place, meeting lots of new people in our community. It can feel exhausting and discouraging when the rejections come in a blank stare or a polite "thank-you, but no-thank-you" reply. But perhaps we can hear some good news from the example of Jesus. Finding receptive people requires broad and extensive seed-scattering. Open-minded, curious people are out there. The COVID-19 pandemic has elevated spiritual curiosity online, and many planters are authentically engaging new people there. That said, we cannot force readiness. We do well to preserve our emotional reserves when the field is rocky.

Failing to follow Jesus in this practice is the cause for much frustration in church planting. When we sow narrowly and expect receptivity, we usually are in for a small harvest. One of the mistakes we make is to expect unreceptive people to become receptive on our time schedule. That rarely takes place. The better investment is to find new people into which we sow. In that, we must make careful choices. One church planter chose to work as a local ski instructor, only to find that very few of those coming for training were even remotely from the community he was planting in. It was a great place to meet new people but not a strategic place to meet the people in his community. By contrast, another planter linked up with a volunteer local hospital as a chaplain in their community. There, he had occasion to connect and pray with individuals and families at critical times. In that effort, he met many who were receptive to conversations around learning spiritual practices to help them manage stress and anxiety. Another planter became the chaplain for the local police department and spent one night each week riding around town, meeting all kinds of people in all kinds of predicaments. Receptivity was regularly the response when these two planters made their respective rounds.

Jesus was in search of the receptive people because he knew they were out there. To find them, we must move and initiate widely. We may also need to make wise strategic choices. The good news Jesus has for us is that some will indeed respond, if we plant as he did.

Reflect: How are you mirroring the "place to place" style of Jesus? Where might you be expecting readiness yet finding disinterest and thus in need of changing your strategy? What new places might the Spirit of Jesus be leading you to visit and scatter seed?

Prayer: *Lord of the harvest, thank you for the example you have given me as a seeker of receptivity. Give me the energy and patience to sow the seeds of your kingdom today in the lives of new people. Thank you for the promise that some are ready to receive. Amen.*

※ 9 ※

IT'S ALL ABOUT RELATIONSHIPS

Read Luke 10:38-42.

> *"Martha, Martha," the Lord answered, "you are worried and upset about many things, but few things are needed—or indeed only one. Mary has chosen what is better, and it will not be taken away from her."*
>
> —Luke 10:41-42

The story of Jesus and his visit to the home of Mary and Martha is a window into the practice of hospitality in the first century. Making room for guests was highly valued. Part of that virtue probably included preparing a meal; arranging a room; making up a bed; and, of course, cleaning up from the activities of the day. Martha has plenty to do and is pulled in different directions in her efforts to cover all those bases. As the logistics person in the family, she has her hands full. In exasperation, Martha finally speaks out, asking Jesus to talk with her sister, recruiting her for the household duties of hospitality to which Mary seems to be oblivious.

Mary, by contrast, shows another side of hospitality—"the better part," according to Jesus. She sits with the guest, Jesus, and is rather unconcerned with the mechanics of his visit. She pays attention to her visitor and gives Jesus the full gift of her undivided attention and conversation. The contrast of these two sisters is classic. One is a doer, and the other is a relator. The problem that Jesus identifies with Martha is not her serving but rather that she is distracted or *periespato,* in Greek, which carries with it the connotation of being pulled in many directions. Her task list is becoming an end unto itself, such that she is missing the opportunity to engage with Jesus personally. It's hard not to be sympathetic toward Martha while we hear the wisdom of Jesus to the sisters.

I recently worked with a planter who impressed me with his growing self-awareness in this area. Jim had been an overachiever in his college and seminary days, reaching valedictorian status. He also was a distance runner, which kept him on a fairly strict training routine. He shared with me how he had become aware of the way his past experience oriented him toward accomplishing the tasks of ministry. He had tended to approach things with a driven, Type A personality style. Now, with a deep apprecia-tion for the importance of relational skills, he had learned to temper his approach to tasks, making considerable effort to develop his relational side. He worked on the "soft skills" of establishing trust, developing moti-vation, promoting teamwork, practicing effective communication skills, showing leadership, and navigating personalities. One particularly smart thing he did early on in his ministry was opening his home with his wife often to people as a signal of their desire to be in relationship beyond the "business" of ministry. That act, along with other intentional efforts, sent a strong message that he wanted a relationship that went beyond just achieving his ministry objectives.

Church planters carry a long list of necessary duties and benchmarks that call for their time and attention. Like Martha, they are pulled in many directions. My Type A pastor friend told me about a major commu-nity fundraising event they had pulled off. It had been full of the potential for being pulled in many directions by many distractions. We both agreed that had he been less aware of his natural orientation toward tasks, he may not have made the concerted effort to make new relational connec-tions through that event, knowing that in the long run, those relationships would be the essential thing. Relationship skills are at the heart of minis-try, and Jesus calls out this valuable priority and practice in Mary.

The story of Mary and Martha calls us first into relationship with Jesus before we simply do the business of Jesus. The story also under-scores how cultivating strong relationships with people should always be at the center of what we do, as Jesus advises we too should choose "the better part." Many of us have encountered Dale Carnegie's book *How to* Win Friends and Influence People at some point in our learning (with more than 30 million copies having been sold worldwide). We may be wise to pick up this classic and review the time-tested insights within its pages. What Carnegie makes clear is that growing relationships in connection with any venture—profit or nonprofit—requires wisdom, and that intentional practices can make all the difference.[1]

Beginning with self-awareness like my friend Jim, we do well to consciously develop the habits of relational leadership. We grow in that when we take a genuine interest in others, learn to talk about issues they deeply care about, ask more questions, practice the give and take of conversational skills, remember names and the stories behind the faces we connect with, and slow down our interactions. Our nonverbal communications can be a big part of that also, including eye contact and body language.

Jesus saw relational priority and skill in Mary that he practiced himself, and he names that authentic style for our benefit. Relational skills are integral to planting like Jesus.

Reflect: What is your natural orientation—toward relationship or toward tasks? What feedback might you seek to grow in this area? What small steps could you take to deepen relationships with people around you?

Prayer: *Lord of this new day, with many duties and tasks, give me a fresh awareness of myself in relationship to others around me. Help me to "choose the better" when there are so many competing things for my attention, I pray. Amen.*

❊ 10 ❊

PARTIES ARE MAGNETS

Read Matthew 9:9-12.

> *While Jesus was having dinner at Matthew's house, many tax collectors and sinners came and ate with him and his disciples.*

—Matthew 9:10

Church planting is highly relational work. If you are not always good at connecting with new people in ways that build a bridge, consider the practices of Jesus. He is a master at relationships, including building bridges with new people.

First, Jesus is out and about in the places where people are doing their routine business when he meets up with Matthew. We can say this because tax collectors set up their booths at places of import and export, where customs or tolls would be charged upon merchants who came to buy or sell in Judea. Picture Jesus at the local marketplace in your community: Notice how he moves with people who may not typically socialize with a carpenter or a budding preacher. The little we know of Matthew suggests that this tax collector had not been experiencing abundant life in his work. He was likely a Jew (his name was Levi; the name Matthew would actually come later), and he had the unenviable occupation of collecting money that went to Rome. Imagine looking your neighbors in the eye when you made a transaction with them as you represented an occupying foreign government. Levi was prime for an excuse to walk off his job into something, most anything, different. Then one day, Jesus enters into Matthew's world, making a timely connection. Game on!

With a new follower, Jesus might have proceeded to a predictable place, such as the home of one of his close disciples; or he might simply have taken Matthew on the road with him. However, that would have begun to cut Matthew off from his old circles of friends. Instead, Jesus forms enough of a connection to share a meal at Matthew's home with those former associates. Together, Jesus and Matthew invite the disciples, plus a bunch of Matthew's old "IRS" cronies, for a night to remember. Some of those associations were not particularly reputable. Imagine the spirit of that gathering—an office retirement party for Matthew, where everyone celebrated the years that they had together working in the tax business and wishing Matthew well in his new adventure. The mood was probably jubilant, as Matthew would now be free of his old Roman boss, and they all could not help but toast the news. It was probably a magnetic moment when the drudgery of life lifted a bit and people could embrace friendships, transitions, and good food and drink. The text shows us Jesus right where he wanted to be, in the middle of that experience with those people. Imagine the moment when Matthew's friends asked him exactly what he planned to do next; imagine how that party must have created a moment they all would not quickly forget as Matthew announced he was going on the road with Jesus.

My wife and I are a clergy couple. You can guess the looks on faces when the people in our neighborhood learned that bit of our bio. So, we broke the ice by hosting a neighborhood BBQ on our front driveway a few years ago. During the holidays, we routinely throw open the doors of our home for a neighborhood open house, with lots of food and drink; and in the summer, we have opened our deck and pool for a neighborhood hangout. Our neighbors always come, appreciative that someone took the initiative to host a party. Recently, a neighbor reciprocated by inviting us to a Euchre card party with all their work colleagues on a Saturday night, which did not finally wind down until well after midnight. Of course, everyone had to make a joke about the preacher sleeping through church the next day! Friendships form, people drop their guard, and conversations get past "the weather" in those parties. We get to be real humans, and our neighbors feel a bit less awkward around the clergy couple in the neighborhood.

So much of life, for so many people, is a challenge, either to get through school or to find a job or to hold on to that job or to raise kids or to mow the lawn or to manage a million mundane tasks. The routine can drain away much of the joy. With the reality of God's in-breaking kingdom of grace and hope, there is good reason to punctuate all those routines with parties. Take a lesson from Jesus: People rarely can resist a good celebration!

Reflect: Where do you see people under the weight of their routines and challenges? What occasion is available for you to throw a party? Who are the "disciples" and "tax collectors" you should invite?

Prayer: *God of all that is good, thank you for the reasons your kingdom gives us to celebrate with others. Help me to show others your great love and the coming kingdom banquet party through gatherings of people who need to know your grace through Jesus. Amen.*

— 11 —

JESUS' SUCCESS STRATEGY

Read John 15:1-17.

> "I am the vine; you are the branches. If you remain in me
> and I in you, you will bear much fruit; apart from me you
> can do nothing."
>
> —John 15:5

Because church planting can be so hard, it is understandable that many of us go looking to podcasts, books, seminars, and training events to help us succeed. Those are usually well and fine, so long as we do not lose sight of Jesus. The success strategy he offers is to "remain in me and I in you." That is to say, Jesus provides more than the message for church planting. He provides our best method. He gives us the ministry strategy that produces fruitfulness, and we are wise to always check ourselves and the teachings we receive against him. So what does it mean to remain in Jesus?

For starters, Jesus meant that we should carry his message: "If you remain in me and my words remain in you . . ." (v. 7). Jesus' message was that God's kingdom was present in him and in his ministry (see Mark 1:14-15). He also meant that *remaining* would include our keeping his command to love (John 15:9-12). Carrying the message of the kingdom and demonstrating that message in love of God and neighbor are two direct ways Jesus teaches, in John 15, whereby we abide in him. Robert E. Logan identifies several incarnational practices from Jesus that help us think further about remaining in Jesus in his book *The Missional Journey*:

Multiplying Disciples and Churches That Transform the World.[1] Let's consider some of these practices of Jesus.

Start with the example Jesus set of deeply connecting with people and with the predicament they faced. He did not stand at a distance but touched, walked with, visited, listened to, and ate with people wherever they were. He had feelings of compassion (see Matthew 9:35-36). He especially cared for the least and last in his world. Remaining in Jesus certainly includes that authentic engagement with people (see Luke 8:1-3). Notice how he is fully present with each individual he meets while he also has the capacity to teach a crowd. While Jesus was fully engaged with people in whatever setting, he was also fully committed to a greater mission directed by his Father (see John 4:34). Remaining in Jesus would then include living purposefully into the mission of God. We would certainly say that Jesus continually called people to follow him and to be in relationship with the Father in heaven and on a journey of discipleship. So we would conclude that remaining in him includes making new disciples and staying connected to our Father in heaven.

Jesus' recommendation for remaining in him (or "abiding in him," as the King James Version translates it) to bear fruit that lasts is no mystery. We could summarize this, as Robert Logan has, under the following five practices: (1) Carry the message of the kingdom; (2) live the command to love; (3) authentically engage people in their predicament; (4) pursue the mission of God purposefully; and (5) call others to follow Jesus, as we ourselves stay connected to God.[2] Each of these principles must be applied to our specific planting context and world, but they all are workable ways we can abide in Jesus.

Jeb is a planter friend working in urban Chicago. From his own experience as an immigrant, he knew the challenges of adapting to a new country. He felt deeply the burden of those who had made this enormous transition. So, every week he arranged to provide a meal for many Indian immigrant people who were scattered and struggling to make their way in a new country. As he worked to authentically engage with people in their predicament and as he showed them love, people were drawn to him. The relationships built and the meals shared became a lifegiving experience for people wrestling to rebuild their lives. In time, they would hear of his purposeful mission to invite them into the kingdom of Jesus. Jeb faced many challenges in his planting work, but he moved forward with clarity and conviction because he was abiding in Jesus.

Most of us would agree that the measure of our success is faithfulness. The question that may remain, however, is, "Faithful to what?" Being faithful to an ecclesiastical system or to a particular community can be a very honorable objective and may be part of a successful ministry, but surely there is more. The challenge that Jesus gives is for us to be faithful to him and his incarnational example. This is at the core of planting like Jesus.

Reflect: After pondering the call of Jesus to "remain in me," how do you hear him calling you to a deeper presence with him? Which of the five practices shared might he be leading you to cultivate more deeply? How does this help you measure your progress?

Prayer: *Lord Jesus, I seek to walk closely with you, to remain connected to you, and to abide in your way. In the many voices I hear that direct me in my ministry, help me to hear yours above all, calling me into your way and your design for my life and work. I pray, in your name. Amen.*

❋ 12 ❋

EATING AND DRINKING

Read Luke 15:1-7.

> *"The Son of Man came eating and drinking, and you say,*
> *'Here is a glutton and a drunkard, a friend of tax collectors*
> *and sinners."*

—Luke 7:34

"Never eat lunch alone" is common advice for people in business. Mealtimes create space for conversations that often integrate the most important things in life. We come for a meal and end up discussing our families, business, the latest news, our plans for the weekend, and our hopes for the future. Little wonder that Jesus came "eating and drinking." Much of what he did to engage people happened over food. Luke's Gospel identifies at least ten meals where Jesus leveraged the table for his mission.[1] Stop and consider how these mealtime practices could be important to recover in pioneer start-up work today.

First, Jesus used mealtimes to build bridges with those who were most despised (see Luke 5:27-32). Levi was a loan shark and an opponent of the people of God. The meal Jesus shares with him elicits a strong reaction from the religious establishment. Imagine inviting those who are most opposed to faith-based efforts in your community to share a meal!

Second, Jesus used mealtimes to meet people who were outside of his normal circles (see Luke 7:36-38). He had no idea a woman "who lived a sinful life" would show up at that Pharisee's house uninvited

(v. 37). Imagine the relationship possibilities when we accept an invitation to share a meal with new people.

Third, Jesus provided meals for those who were hungry. Seeing a large, hungry crowd, he instructs his disciples to feed them (see Luke 9:10-17). Meeting the basic needs of an individual or a group opens the door for conversation. Whom around us can we personally serve in their most basic need for food?

Fourth, Jesus used mealtimes to go deeper in relationships (see Luke 10:38-42). Busy lives leave people relationally hungry. Mealtimes are occasions to come together for one another. Think of someone whose life seems a blur and meet that person for breakfast.

Fifth, Jesus used mealtimes to teach powerfully (see Luke 11:37-53). A question posed over food leads to a memorable lesson. Might the table be the right place at times for teaching? What if you launched your public worship over a Sunday brunch?

Sixth, Jesus knew that table conversations could become controversial (see Luke 14:1-24). Debatable topics are not uncommon at mealtimes. How can they be handled in ways that draw people in rather than push them away?

Seventh, Jesus used mealtimes to tell his signature stories (see Luke 15:1-7). Imagine everyone with their mouths full and Jesus holding their attention with a parable. Might our best stories and lessons be reserved for those moments of table silence?

Eighth, Jesus saw the loners and outcasts and used mealtimes to form relationships (see Luke 19:1-10). What a simple pleasure, to not eat alone. Imagine offering that simple request to share a meal to solitary souls.

Ninth, Jesus saw the immense spiritual potential that exists around a meal (see Luke 22:14-38). The Last Supper would forever be etched in their minds with the lessons of service and sacrifice Jesus gave. Imagine providing spiritual and physical food together for hungry people.

Tenth, Jesus used mealtimes to develop disciples (see Luke 24:28-32). The simple acts of being with his disciples and breaking bread while studying the scriptures transformed them. Imagine the slower pace of a meal to reflect upon the word.

Verlon Fosner, in his book *Dinner Church: Building Bridges by Baking Bread*, reminds us that church today did not always look this way. Straight rows, passive listening, parading in and out through the doors is not the how the early church formed. They gathered over meals and in homes. The pace of the meal created a structure for their worship.[2] Little wonder that the dinner table is being rediscovered as a place where church can come to be. Food was integral to faith formation in the early church. We can find references to the "love feast" in Jude 1:12 and references to communal meals in 1 Corinthians 11:17 and following.

In these ways, the members of the early church were following the pattern of Jesus, who sought out table conversation for his teaching. From that place, he ministered to his disciples, to religious leaders, and to those who were on the fringe. Those experiences were profoundly influential and winsome in their time, as they can be today. For these reasons, eating and drinking with people at table is a big part of planting like Jesus.

Reflect: Which table practice of Jesus do you feel prompted to closely follow? What dimensions of your ministry might you position or need to reposition around a meal? Whom might you include in table gatherings who otherwise might remain on the fringe or outside your ministry?

Prayer: *Lord Jesus, just as you met with people at table in your ministry, help me use your provision of food and drink to feed people in body and soul. Show me how to build bridges for your Spirit through breaking bread. I pray, in your name. Amen.*

✵ 13 ✵

GOSPEL OPTIMISM

Read Matthew 13:31-32; Luke 15:11-32.

> *Then Jesus asked, "What is the kingdom of God like? What shall I compare it to? It is like a mustard seed, which a man took and planted in his garden. It grew and became a tree, and the birds perched in its branches."*
>
> —Luke 13:18-19

Evangelistic optimism is a predictor of evangelistic success. As you might imagine, if we believe that the gospel has the power to transform lives, it is much more likely that we will share the gospel with confidence, expecting a positive outcome. That optimism springs from the mouth of Jesus, who said his kingdom is like a tiny mustard seed that grows and grows (see Matthew 13:31-32). When we form an authentic relationship with trust and common ground, we can confidently share with another person our experience with Jesus. Sharing that story, it is entirely possible that someone may suspend their unbelief or indifference, even if just for a moment, and open themselves to Christ. In his book *Evangelism in a Skeptical World: How to Make the Unbelievable News About Jesus More Believable,* Sam Chan identifies three biblical pictures of gospel witness that promote the optimistic outlook Jesus had.[1]

First, when Jesus tells the story of the prodigal son (see Luke 15:11-32), he paints a profile of a person who is willfully rejecting God. We can feel the harshness of that broken relationship as the son demands his inheritance, as if to say he wishes his father were dead. The trajectory of this son is entirely away from home and from his father until there comes a day of crisis. He comes to the end of himself, which leads to an awakening: His life would be better if he were home. Today, a significant segment of North America would say they are done with church. We might say that Jesus is describing these "dones" in this story. Engaging a person who is hostile to faith is likely to require much patience until circumstances crack the hardened shell of resistance. Still, the big picture Jesus paints is an optimistic one of reunion and reconciliation.

Second, consider Luke's telling of the story of Saul, the religious zealot and persecutor of the early church. Coupled with his remarkable spiritual transformation story, Saul-turned-Paul is a profile very different from the prodigal son (see Acts 9:1-19). Saul meticulously fulfills all of his religious duties and obligations to win favor with God, until a dramatic encounter with Jesus, where he is forced to reconsider his religious assumptions. In North America today, many people would say they are Christian (particularly if today were their wedding day or funeral) but that they do not regularly attend worship. For many of these "cultural Christians," they are living decent lives with the assumption that in the end, God will weigh out their behavior on moral scales. The optimistic picture we get from Paul's life is that the amazing grace of God in Jesus can awaken an authentic encounter with Jesus that is truly transformational. When an individual grasps the radical nature of grace, understanding that following Jesus is more than a commitment to "clean up your life," watch out!

Finally, consider the story of the church in Sardis (see Revelation 3: 1-6). Here is a whole group of people who may have thought of themselves as spiritually alive but who were actually "dead" (v. 1). This group may have been smaller in the first century, but their counterparts today appear to include a very large sector of North America. These are the people we meet who, when asked, say they worship—but in reality, that is one or two weekends a year. Why don't they attend church regularly? There are many reasons, too many to try to list here. For many of them, however, their experience with Christ has only been formal, ritualistic, or simply unremarkable. "Wake up!" is the hope John has for them and the hope we have for our de-churched or under-churched friends. They may know of

Jesus but need to hear a fresh invitation to commitment to follow him as their Savior and Lord.

In planting, we look for receptivity with optimistic eyes. Sharing our experience with Jesus often cuts through the static and the skepticism. We can witness to how he gives purpose, forgiveness, hope, healing, and community. We can tell our authentic story. The Spirit of God will use that story in the lives of the de-churched, under-churched, or anti-church people. That awakening Spirit is always ahead of us, at work generating spiritual life even in the lives of the most unlikely people. Moving with that attitude of hope is part of planting like Jesus.

Reflect: How optimistic would you say you tend to be as it relates to evangelistic efforts? Which of the three biblical types outlined above do you feel most closely reflects the people you are engaging? How do the biblical types give you insight into sharing Jesus?

Prayer: *God, sometimes life, with its challenges and routine, weighs people down. Thank you, that the good news of your kingdom meets people where they are with hope. Use my life to show your goodness, love, and grace to those I seek to build bridges with. In Jesus' name. Amen.*

✳ 14 ✳

ASKING QUESTIONS

Read Matthew 6:26-30; 16:13-16.

> *"Who do people say that the Son of Man is?" And they said, "Some say John the Baptist, but others Elijah, and still others Jeremiah or one of the prophets." He said to them, "But who do you say that I am?"*
>
> —Matthew 16:13-15, NRSV

Effective leaders draw others deeply into their vision by asking great questions. Socrates made much of this method in his teaching in the fifth century before Christ. Jesus is the model for this principle in his own time, as the Gospels together record more than one hundred questions that he posed to people in various places. In fact, it seems there was hardly any interaction of Jesus (either one on one, with disciples or skeptics, or with crowds or small groups) where he did not use questions to deliver his impact.

Let's consider just a few of Jesus' thought-provoking questions: Why are you afraid? Do you believe I can do this? Who do you say that I am? Does this offend you? Do you want to be made well? What is written in the law . . . how do you understand it? Do you love me? What is that to you? Do you believe this? What are you looking for? Does this teaching surprise you? Do you want to leave me? What are you discussing? Why do you judge for yourself what is right? Do you still not understand? Why are you so anxious? Who do you say that I am?[1] Add them all up, and we can see how Jesus favored this tool. Leaders in the field of business agree on how powerful questions can be to unlock learning and draw people together.[2] Jesus checks all the boxes when it comes to fully leveraging questions to help achieve his mission. He asks many questions; he often uses follow-up questions; he knows when to keep questions open-ended; and he knows when to ask the hardest question first. When Jesus asks a question, sometimes it is rhetorical and sometimes it is not, but every time, it draws people into relationship with him in a new way. He will not settle for passive listeners.

Jeremy knew he needed to engage people in his community deeply, given that he was virtually "parachuting in" with little preexisting support. Beginning with a community survey and door-to-door conversations, he started: "How long have you lived here? What do you like about this community? What concerns you about this place? Can we stay in touch?" It was a simple series of questions that initiated relationship and sent a strong message that he wanted to listen. In that process, he was looking not only for answers to the questions but also for who engaged most eagerly. Those were the folks he made plans to follow up with and invite into further conversation. Crowdsourcing, the practice of drawing out field insights from a large number of people to design an effort, is all about asking the right questions in the right way. Jeremy maintained his open posture by posting his survey questions online, where he consistently directed the people he networked with. Over time, he developed a remarkable range of insight into his community while also forming many relationships with interested people. Good questions deliver on so many levels.

Another reason why the example of Jesus in this area is essential as a planting tool relates to developing people to their potential. Whether we are discipling a new believer or coaching a new key leader, good questions help people slow down to reflect upon their circumstances or their leadership challenge, consider their options, and make intentional choices. "What do you think you should do in this situation?" is the type of question, when accompanied by other related questions and with patient listening, that helps someone think things through and then take responsibility for their choices. Most people will breathe an inner sigh of relief when we hold back our opinions and recommendations and instead, lead with a good question.

Jesus' practice of asking powerful questions reaches a peak in Matthew 16, when he asks Peter and the other disciples, "Who do you say that I am?" Given the many "I am" statements he makes (see John 6:35; 8:12; 10:9; 11:25; 14:6; and 15:5) and Peter's reply, it is clear that Jesus is interested in how people assess his identity and mission. His practice of asking questions is often tied to his desire to create a moment of decision in his followers. The questions we ask can do the same.

Questions help us to advance the kingdom mission and develop people to their potential. On the surface, it sounds simple; but down deep, good questions help us plant like Jesus.

Reflect: How effective are you in asking thought-provoking questions? What questions might you need to ask in your current interactions with people? Where should you be asking questions and listening more while speaking less?

Prayer: *Thank you, Jesus, for the many examples you have given us of your skillful use of questions with others. As you used this tool to advance your mission and develop people to their full potential, help me to ask questions and then listen more often. I pray, in your name. Amen.*

❋ 15 ❋

DISCIPLESHIP RHYTHMS

Read Matthew 16:13-27.

> *Then Jesus said to his disciples, "Whoever wants to be my disciple must deny themselves and take up their cross and follow me. For whoever wants to save their life will lose it, but whoever loses their life for me will find it."*
>
> —Matthew 16:24-25

Jesus is Lord" is the earliest confession of the church. More than just a Savior from sin and guilt or a ticket to the happy hereafter, Jesus asserts his rightful rulership over every aspect of our lives. In Matthew 16, Jesus states in vivid terms what is required to follow him. It is a picture of our own crucifixion as we "take up our cross." So often, that phrase is associated with some misfortune in life: "That is their cross to bear." But for Jesus, our cross is not a misfortune that regrettably falls upon us. No, it is a decision to obey Jesus that we willingly "take up." It's our choice. Leading people into that practice is much of what making disciples is all about. Look closely at how Jesus makes disciples.

In Matthew's account of Jesus with Peter and the other disciples, there is a noticeable cycle of what Mike Breen has identified to be "invitation and challenge" in his book *Building a Discipling Culture: How to Release a Missional Movement by Discipling People Like Jesus Did*.[1] First, Jesus invites Peter into a close relationship with him over the years they are together, leading up to a remarkable episode in Matthew 16. There, he names Peter as a rock on which the church will be built, and he offers the keys to the kingdom, a significant position of authority: "I will give you the keys of the kingdom of heaven" (Matt. 16:19). This all adds up to high invitation for Peter.

What follows in the story in verses 20 through 27 is a bit of a shocker, as Jesus lays out his intention to go to Jerusalem to suffer and die and then triumph in resurrection, to which Peter objects. Jesus replies strongly, challenging Peter to get his perspective and values in check: "You only have human concerns on your mind, not God's concerns" (v. 23, AP). Jesus continues, with a dense teaching on self-denial and losing your life. Imagine Peter trying to wrap his mind around this difficult saying from Jesus and how he would live into it all. This all adds up to a high challenge for Peter. What we can see in this exchange with Peter is Jesus demonstrating for us his rhythm of high invitation followed by high challenge.

Jason is following this rhythm of high invitation and high challenge with the men he is engaging in his planting work. He schedules monthly events that are easy to invite guys to, including axe throwing and a daddy-daughter Valentine's Day dance. Other guys, he invites to join him in community-impact projects where they engage local needs in an environment of fun and local collaboration. Parallel to those opportunities, Jason has launched several high-commitment discipleship groups modeled on the Wesleyan covenant "band model." In those groups, the values of scripture study and personal accountability are strong. Jason's pattern of high invitation and high commitment is growing the discipleship culture he desires in his start-up.

This rhythm of high invitation and high commitment is not the only cycle that we can observe in Jesus' practice. We also know that there were places where he chose to spend more time (the region of Galilee, for example) and places where he limited his exposure (most certainly Jerusalem), until the time came to change that pattern (see Luke 9:51). Jesus recognized that some people were receptive to his message, while others were disinterested or resistant, and he advised his disciples to pay attention to that reality (see Matthew 10:14). We planters often recognize these same rhythms of receptivity and resistance in our work, as an individual or community may not always be receptive to our efforts for reasons beyond our control. In those circumstances, we must move on and cultivate other places that are more open until circumstances change.

Jesus is a master at developing a discipleship culture, moving Peter and his partners along on a path of deeper commitment. He draws his followers close, spending time with them over meals, during travels, and in daily routines, allowing them access to him. Jesus also challenges them deeply to take radical new steps of personal change and obedience to his mission. In so doing, he shows us the rhythms of discipleship.

Finally, it is worth reminding us that the most effective practice of this cycle of invitation and challenge is done one on one. Jesus certainly invites and challenges the masses, but he usually focuses his discipleship rhythms upon a few. His dialogue with Peter in Matthew 16 is an example. When invitation and challenge is heard by a crowd, individuals can deflect it; the impact can be lost. But when the high invitation and high challenge is one on one, it is much harder to deflect or avoid. Jesus, through his invitation-challenge interchanges with Peter and with many other individuals in the Gospels, gives us a compelling picture of his disciple-making practice.

Reflect: How intentional are you in your relationships with those you want to disciple? How might you practice the rhythms of high invitation and high challenge with those individuals? Where do you see receptivity and resistance in your work, and how might that guide you in future efforts?

Prayer: *Jesus, I thank you for your example of invitation and challenge. Show me who I am being led to invite into a closer relationship and make it clear by your Spirit how I am to challenge them to follow you more closely, I pray. Amen.*

❊ 16 ❊

SOCIAL TRANSFORMATION

Read Luke 4:18-19; Acts 19:1-41.

> *"The Spirit of the Lord is on me,*
> *because he has anointed me*
> *to proclaim good news to the poor.*
> *He has sent me to proclaim freedom for the prisoners*
> *and recovery of sight for the blind,*
> *to set the oppressed free,*
> *to proclaim the year of the Lord's favor."*
>
> —Luke 4:18-19

Alyssa was planting in an oil boomtown in the western Dakotas that had sprung up like a weed as a result of new petroleum-extraction methods and higher crude market prices. The runaway growth in that town had created many problems, not the least being skyrocketing housing costs and illicit drug use. The negative impact of that dynamic upon individuals and families was pervasive. It was impossible to plant in that community without encountering the pain and brokenness that had devastated lives. It was also impossible to plant in that community without facing and challenging the greed and abusive systems that took advantage of vulnerable people. Alyssa had her hands full, and her example illustrates the need for the whole gospel to address the whole person.

In the earliest phase of his public ministry, Jesus announced his mission to bring good news to the poor, the prisoners, the blind, and the oppressed. As he moved out in his mission into towns and villages, our

Lord faced great suffering and struggle arising from systemic oppression. In the Gospels, for example, we see Jesus repeatedly addressing the abusive system of patriarchy (see John 8:1-11; Luke 8:1-3). We see how he treated women with dignity and respect. His example keeps us mindful of the profound impact the kingdom message has, yet today.

Acts 19 records another dramatic picture of oppression in Ephesus, the site of the temple of Artemis, one of the Seven Wonders of the Ancient World. Travelers to that temple would purchase silver shrines of the Greek goddess, and this trade had become a source of considerable local revenue. When Paul arrives, he first engages with new people and sees them profess Jesus. Then, after a demonstration of spiritual power, more people profess Christ and renounce their practice of sorcery, taking active steps of discipleship. Seeing the power of the Spirit at work in new believers, Paul publicly declares that the worship of the goddess Artemis is a sham, and in so doing, he threatens the income the silversmiths have been gaining from the visiting tourists. Fortunately, a city clerk quiets the reactive uproar with an appeal to the rule of law.

Acts 19 is not the only example of a church planter running into structural powers that are in need of transformation. Acts 16 records an incident in Philippi wherein Paul again bumps up against people who are profiteering from an abusive practice—in this case, a possessed fortune-telling girl who is enslaved and whose abilities are exploited by her owners (see vv. 16-18). Paul's involvement there got him thrown into prison, which ultimately led to some of the first converts to the church plant in Philippi.

From each of these stories, it is clear that early church planters did not shy away from following Jesus in addressing the social structures, systems, and powers that were in opposition to the gospel. It is also important to note that in both stories, there are examples of people who are changing their personal beliefs and attitudes. The change that Paul pursued in the abusive systems he faced was not apart from his desire to see individual transformation. It might even be said that individual transformations of beliefs and attitudes were the tipping point.

Today, sociologists who think about cultural change and health interventions refer to levels of influence in that process as the "social ecological model." Total transformation, they say, requires as many as five dimensions being addressed, including the individual dimension; the interpersonal dimension; the community dimension; the institutional dimension; and, ultimately, the policy dimension.[1] The gospel of Jesus has a redemptive message for each of these domains. As leaders in the kingdom movement of Jesus, we follow his practice of giving great attention to the individual beliefs and interpersonal behaviors and attitudes leading to the formation of a countercultural community, while at the same time we are neither unaware nor neglectful of the larger systems, powers, and principalities. Planting like Jesus means that we announce his kingdom to be over all things.

Reflect: Where do you see the systems and structures of sin and injustice in your community? Where might God be leading you to pray, engage, serve, or speak? Who are the people who are being negatively impacted by these oppressive systems?

Prayer: *Lord of all that is right and good, I pray that your kingdom would come with power and authority in my community to bring justice and mercy. Show me how I best do the whole work of the gospel in this place. Amen.*

✵ 17 ✵

LOVING PEOPLE

Read Luke 10:25-37.

> *"Love the Lord your God with all your heart and with all your soul and with all your strength and with all your mind'; and, 'Love your neighbor as yourself.'"*

—Luke 10:27

If you have ever asked yourself who and how often you should love another person, Bob Goff has an answer. Bob writes a lot about love. In his book *Everybody, Always: Becoming Love in a World Full of Setbacks and Difficult People*, he talks about his desire to love "everybody, always—and start with the people who creep us out."[1] Goff's book is an inspiring portrayal of what love can look like when it is practiced in everyday life, for everyday people.

The way that Jesus has for us is marked by love. Jesus said so much about love that it is both overwhelming to take in and disarmingly simple. The greatest commandment is to love. The greatest witness to the world is love. The sign of our love for Jesus is to follow and keep his commands. The greatest love is to lay down one's life for others. It would make perfect sense for Jesus to have said that church planting is a labor of love. Let's look a bit closer at one love episode from Jesus' teachings, one that has particular relevance for planting pioneers.

When Jesus told the parable of the good Samaritan to a lawyer who was concerned about his keeping the law of love, he outlined a study in contrasts. Jesus' story opens with a Jewish man who is traveling between Jericho and Jerusalem and is ambushed by bandits. A Samaritan who was culturally distant (Jews and Samaritans had no dealings with one another) but physically close (he passes nearby the man in distress) does the right thing by extending care. The priest and the Levite, on the other hand, are both culturally and physically close, yet in contrast, they could not find it within themselves to extend a hand to a beaten traveler; they had other things to do. After calling out the difference, Jesus tells the lawyer to be like the Samaritan. The teaching is clear: Love can show up when we pay less attention to lifestyle or cultural divides. As Bob Goff says, love is for everybody, always. Jesus demonstrates this same quality of radical love in his encounter with a Canaanite woman who also was a distant outsider (see Matthew 15:21-28).

These stories pack a real punch if you place them next to one frequent area of church-planting design and planning. I am referring to the work most planters do at some point to understand their field demographics. The fields of demographics and marketing studies today tell us that America can be atomized into more than seventy different lifestyle segments.[2] These individual groups have unique consumer preferences and patterns. They cluster into nineteen affinities that share common characteristics.[3] Anticipating needs and preferences is seen as the key to marketing success. Know your customers and target them with laser precision if you want to raise the chances of a desirable response. It all makes perfect sense.

Church planting counsel generally affirms this approach, and there are excellent sources available to leverage demographic insights for planters.[4] When we define who we are trying to reach and then home in on their worship, hospitality, and a dozen other preference distinctives, we increase our potential effectiveness, so the logic goes. While this is certainly not all bad, it can position us perilously close to that priest and that Levite and a long way from the "everybody, always" way of Jesus. We may find ourselves passing by a person in distress because we are in a hurry to reach our select group. This is definitely not planting like Jesus.

No ministry can be all things to all people. We cannot meet every need or respond to every appeal. Even Jesus did not heal everyone. We all must make choices about where and with whom we will spend our time so as to be most effective in our mission field. The diversity and connectivity of our world make this a real challenge.

That said, God will reveal from time to time someone on our path "going down from Jerusalem to Jericho." It may well be someone who does not match our intended focus group. It may be someone who interrupts our busy schedule (such as the person I met this morning on the subway in desperate need of help). In those times, Jesus both demonstrates and teaches us the way of unconditional love.

Planting like Jesus requires that, insofar as we are able, we love everybody, always.

Reflect: How are you doing at practicing the kind of love Jesus demonstrated and taught? Who are those who do not fit your designs but whom God has placed on your path? What might need to change for you to show love more consistently?

Prayer: *Lord of love, show me how your way of unconditional love is never an impediment to my long list of tasks. Help me see those who need your mercy and give me the wisdom to discern how best to show it. Amen.*

⁕ 18 ⁕

HOSPITALITY

Read Matthew 25:35-36; I Peter 4:7-11.

> *"I was hungry and you gave me something to eat, I was thirsty and you gave me something to drink, I was a stranger and you invited me in, I needed clothes and you clothed me, I was sick and you looked after me, I was in prison and you came to visit me."*

> —Matthew 25:35-36

If there is one gift that is critical for church planting, it is the gift of hospitality. More than cardboard cookies and weak church coffee, hospitality is a profound biblical practice of making space for outsiders. Hospitality flips predictable church upside down in favor of the disconnected and the person on the spiritual fringes. In fact, the ideal first partners in start-up work are people with the gift of hospitality. They will throw a Christmas party for their neighbors, adopt a refugee family, open their home for a dinner book club, or work on learning the names of the new people they meet. Hospitality is a game changer. It always has been, as far back as you look.

In the Old Testament, the people of Israel were commanded to make space for outsiders, including foreigners and immigrants, as a witness to their own experience in Egypt (see Deuteronomy 10:17-19; Leviticus 19:34). Loving the outsider and the "stranger" or "foreigner" was an explicit command. In the New Testament, that value was carried forward, as we are commanded to show hospitality toward the stranger and the outsider (see Hebrews 13:1-2). Jesus points to himself as the "stranger whom you invited in" (Matt. 25:35, adapted). In 1 Peter 4:9, there is the call to offer hospitality without grumbling, expecting nothing in return. Hospitality is about making room for new people, unfamiliar people, people who currently do not quite fit in, so that they can find a place at the table of Jesus. We do this because we too once were strangers and misfits to the kingdom. Hospitality is about putting ourselves in the place of the outsiders and asking, "How can I help them feel at home as they consider Jesus?"

The Greek word that we translate as hospitality is the word *philoxenia*. It actually means "to love (*philo*) the outsider (*xenia*)"—and church planting is all about that, for sure. One of the fun things I get to do is to watch church planters show that love to outsiders. I have great admiration when I see Chris walk alongside people in recovery as one who himself is recovering. In that personal transparency and recovery ministry development, he makes space for outsiders to feel comfortable with Jesus. I have great admiration when I see Josh hanging out with thrash metal band friends and taking that style into his ministry. In his artistic choices, he makes space for outsiders to feel comfortable with Jesus. I have great admiration when I see Gordon striking out into a new fledgling community, setting up and tearing down his worship equipment each week in the local middle school so he can make space for new people in a new community to find Jesus. I have great admiration when I think of Whitney, making space for young families as she plants in a neighborhood with dozens of kids; and Shawn, making space for racial diversity as he forms a multiethnic leadership team to guide his pioneer work; and Tyler, who elevates environmental justice concerns, thereby making room for alienated and offended millennials. I love these leaders because they love outsiders and are willing to go to great ends to show hospitality. They remind us that hospitality values can shape a church plant culture in large and little ways. In fact, we could conclude that our best leadership decisions should bless others with the gift of hospitality.

Hospitality can be expressed at the level of ministry design, as well as in the small gestures and messages we send week in and week out. Hospitality is expressed whenever a leadership team member invites neighbor friends over for BBQ, along with the pastor, as an easy way to spark new relationships; or when a couple makes it their goal to look for visitors every week and not only introduce themselves but also invite these visitors to lunch that very day. In these little acts, we are making relational space for strangers. Who wouldn't want *a dozen* people like those?

Those who will practice hospitality are perhaps the most valuable participants in a new church because they so tangibly show others the way of Jesus, who made space at the table for new people like us. We do well when we encourage this gift and call attention to the gracious practices of hospitality when we see those actions in our team. They are a clear indication that we are indeed planting like Jesus.

Reflect: Whom do you see in your ministry who has a hospitable style that you can lift up as an example? How might you need to model and train this into your team or congregation? How does your ministry carry with it the value of hospitality into every dimension?

Prayer: *Jesus, as you made space for new people in your life, help me to do the same. Guide me in each aspect of my ministry so that I may be as you would be, loving the outsiders and making space for the strangers, that they might find you, I pray. Amen.*

19

TRY AGAIN

Read John 21:1-14.

> *[Jesus] said, "Throw your net on the right side of the boat and you will find some." When they did, they were unable to haul the net in because of the large number of fish.*
>
> —John 21:6

Many times, I have sat with creative, courageous, and faithful leaders during a time of colossal failure. It is no fun. Hindsight is always 20/20, and it pains me to listen patiently as those leaders recount what they could have done better or differently or whatever. Sometimes there are things that are truly within our control that we fail at. Other times, there are things that are truly beyond our control that swamp our boat. Either way, setbacks and failures sting.

In John 21, we come upon the disciples of Jesus on a fishing expedition that is going miserably. They have retreated to their work as fishermen on the heels of the apparent collapse of the Jesus movement following Jesus' crucifixion. Out in the boat all night, they've caught nothing; and now comes the dawn, and they are exhausted. In that moment of maximum discouragement and frustration, they hear the call to throw their nets again, and then comes the remarkable catch. Their eyes are then opened to see Jesus, who has been witness to their worst and best fishing experiences, and the rest of the story is an eruption of celebration, food, and fellowship with Jesus.

In this story, the Gospel writer takes the reader back to the original place where Jesus and the first disciples formed their relationship (see Matthew 4:18-22; Mark 1:16-20; Luke 5:1-11). It was here that Jesus called them to follow and fish in a new way: to make new disciples. That early encounter with Jesus is now fused in John with another event, in which they fish all night and catch nothing, until, as Jesus instructs them, they cast their nets again on the other side of the boat. It is as if the writer is forecasting the "colossal failure" moments that will come in their missionary work (and ours) and the essential response to those moments to "cast again." It is possible to fail backward in utter defeat or we can fail forward, believing we have not yet captured the kingdom catch God has for us. Making new disciples requires many fresh attempts. After a good night's sleep, the sting of setback begins to fade, and we can return to our nets. It is a pattern that shows up at many stages of our work.

Dale was a young visionary leader who felt a call to plant a new church in his hometown. In the early phase, he was significantly challenged by evangelistic practices, though he knew they were essential to start-up work. Dale acknowledged that seminary had distracted him from creatively sharing the good news of Jesus with people in his community. Now, he faced a fresh challenge to "cast again," so he courageously ventured out into his community with a series of missional engagement projects. One was to start a neighborhood Euchre tournament in the gloomy winter months over a series of weekends. There was a significant positive response to his invitation, and during those winter months, Dale formed dozens of new relationships, some of which naturally opened into an occasion for him to build some authentic friendships. In some cases, Dale discovered deeper needs through which he was able to connect and share good news. Long story short, when the day did come that Dale started a new community church in his small town, many of the locals already knew him as a person who was deeply connected with their neighborhoods and who genuinely cared. The net was "cast again," and the catch was significant.

Setbacks and speed bumps are common in church planting. A survey of the book of Acts would include setbacks because of persecution, betrayal, internal conflict, popular resistance, and incarceration; that's not an inspiring list! It has been observed, however, that despite a wide range of setback experiences, the mission of Jesus always seems to advance over the long run. This is the meta-narrative of Acts and of church history. We could say that it is also likely to be our personal narrative and our ministry experience. Setbacks will come. In those moments, Jesus would have us return again to the place he first called us and where he reminds us to stay fishing.

Casting again is a necessary part of planting like Jesus.

Reflect: What recent experience have you had with setback or failure? Has your reaction to that experience kept you from attempting again to fulfill your mission? Why or why not? What do you hear in Jesus' words to his disciples to cast their nets again?

Prayer: *God in heaven, I am in need of extra grace and motivation when my hopes for ministry progress are crushed. Help me believe that you have good purposes beyond my disappointments. Help me always to believe in resurrection through Jesus, I pray. Amen.*

❖ 20 ❖

COMMUNICATION THAT CONNECTS

Read Matthew 5–7; Acts 17:16-34.

> *When Jesus saw the crowds, he went up on a mountainside*
> *and sat down. His disciples came to him, and he began to*
> *teach them.*
>
> —Matthew 5:1-2

As followers of Jesus—"the Word made flesh" (John 1:14, kjv, adapted)—
we have good reason to believe deeply in the power of effective communication to spark transformation. The Word of God in Jesus has been
captured in the scriptures, which then comes alive in our preaching and
teaching as we offer Christ to listeners. In church planting, those listeners are often people who have been distant from organized religion. The
static of their past church experiences, along with a million other distracting events from their last week, becomes like a fog so thick that our
words get lost. How we communicate is a critical factor if we are to keep
them engaged. Words are our most basic tool to work with. How will we
choose them?

In Acts 17, the apostle Paul demonstrates a communication style in
Athens that can be traced directly back to Jesus and the Sermon on the
Mount in Matthew 5–7. Let's look closely. First, Paul connects with his
audience and the circumstances of their lives (see Acts 17:16-21). The
power of that connection is elevated as he is out in the marketplace, where
the Athenians are most comfortable. Jesus did the same when he chose
the relaxed space of a hillside over a stuffy synagogue for his sermon.

We could say that the effectiveness of Jesus and Paul started before they opened their mouths to say anything. Their location and setting gave their message an air of authenticity. This reminds me of those planters who have started a church in a diner or a pub. Many are maximizing Facebook and other social media, where many of the people in our communities already comfortably hang out. Their environment and style communicate that they are down-to-earth and genuine.

After Paul establishes his connection with the people of Athens, he speaks directly to them, affirming their spiritual interest, and then he draws them into his message with a variety of techniques, including story, common illustration, and didactic teaching—all the while, narrowing his focus, until he proclaims Christ. Jesus gives us a broader range of teaching methods, including metaphors and illustrations, rhetorical questions and challenges, in the Sermon on the Mount. Both appeal to a higher authority, leading to a clear focus on Jesus himself (see Acts 17:31; Matthew 7:24). Neither Paul nor Jesus will settle for the listener to just be "a good person"; they want to draw others into an encounter with the person of Jesus himself.

Another way to think about how communicators offer Christ comes from John Wesley, who also connected deeply with his listeners through his open-air meetings. He thought of three ways Jesus is presented: as Prophet (Jesus calling us to believe his teaching), Priest (Jesus calling us to receive his salvation), or King (Jesus calling us to follow his direction).[1] Wesley's guidance can help us think about how we offer Christ and how we call people to decide to follow Christ today. Like Jesus and Paul, John Wesley drew his listeners into a moment of decision, meeting them on their turf, speaking plainly in ways they could understand. That said, he did not fail to ask the discipleship question. It is that call to choose to follow Christ that the Spirit uses to fully do the work of the Word. It is through the mystery of preaching that people suspend their skepticism and believe the good news (see 1 Corinthians 1:21).

Rob is a planter I know who has developed a team of people who understand the principles of effective communication. In developing that team around him, he has opened his message preparation work to them for guidance, wisdom, and support. He calls the process "community preaching." Rob's teammates often help him see the way he is being heard from different perspectives, elevating his effectiveness when it comes to the point of asking people to follow Jesus further. Rob acknowledges that he needs help to be most effective during those critical weekend teaching times. He also feels that some of the weekend preparation burden has been lifted, as he has received much wisdom and insight into both his audience and the texts he teaches. That humility has paid off for him considerably over time.

Giving careful attention to how we message and how listeners will hear us is essential to planting like Jesus.

Reflect: How are you doing at communicating effectively with those you seek to teach in your ministry? What lessons can you take from Jesus and Paul? What might be your next steps? How do you get feedback on your communication effectiveness?

Prayer: *God, I am amazed at the power of your Word. I long for my words to be more effective in the lives of people. Give me your words, so that I might most clearly offer Christ to listeners through my teaching. I pray, for Jesus' sake. Amen.*

Part 2

Daily Readings on Organizational Development Like Jesus

❈ 21 ❈

NEW WINESKINS

Read Mark 2:18-22.

> *"No one pours new wine into old wineskins. Otherwise, the wine will burst the skins, and both the wine and the wineskins will be ruined. No, they pour new wine into new wineskins."*

—Mark 2:21-22

Many of us move into start-up work because we simply believe that the radical good news of Jesus needs a new form or expression for a new place and time. Generations change, and with that change comes a fresh set of circumstances. The past packaging of the gospel may have been effective for an earlier place and time and people, but that cultural wrapper simply does not beg to be opened today. A new form is required today, just as it was in the past.

Mark 2 records an encounter Jesus had with religious leaders who had a cultural wrapper they were committed to in their time and place. The exchange starts around the issue of religious observance of the fast: "How is it that we fast, and you do not?" (Mark 2:18, paraphrased). Or in other words, "What is up with your 'cultural wrapper,' Jesus?" These leaders expect Jesus and his followers to fast in compliance with the Mosaic law. In reply, Jesus draws an analogy I would put like this: "Why fast when a party is in full swing? When I am gone, that is when the fasting can resume" (Mark 2:19-20, paraphrased). In this exchange, Jesus messages a significant change that he represents to the established religious order.

For these religious leaders, Jesus is speaking directly into their blind spot. He is trying to tell them that this is not the time for business as usual; the same old same old will not do. A seismic change is taking place. Then, Jesus shifts the metaphor and drops the hammer. What follows has significant relevance for gospel pioneers.

Old-wineskin religion suffocates the soul: anxiety about living up to expectations, posturing to get credit for good behavior, a daily grind of comparing and competing. Add to that the stuffy exclusivity of religious privilege that dismisses people on the margins. The old system is broken; it cannot be patched up; it will never do. The relentless grace of Jesus does not mix with either a toxic religious system or a vanilla one. This new potent kingdom reality requires a new form. The new wine needs a new wineskin.

The point of this teaching is not missed by spiritual pioneers and entrepreneurs: How we do gospel ministry should not be entirely dictated by an earlier era. While we likely have inherited deep and abiding theological principles and values, the form of our ministry must follow the functions of the kingdom, never the reverse. We must innovate the form afresh for our time and place.

Alan Hirsch memorably expresses this principle in grand terms, advising that our Christology should inform our missiology and our missiology should inform our ecclesiology, never the reverse.[1] We don't start with notions of "church" to be replicated like a cookie cutter but rather we start with Jesus and let him teach us how to do missionary work that yields a faith community that fits the context. So, we applaud a new faith community online or in a laundromat with free washing and worship offered for people in an urban, high-density housing area. How very much like Jesus to meet people where they are, and how delightful it is to see the adaptability of the good news of Jesus to a new time and location.

But might it be that our own frame of mind, our own preconceptions, can become the old wineskin that must be disposed of? Might we be the problem? I once heard a wise planter say that the first or even second drafts of our planting project designs often need to be written out, and then, after we have detailed all the specifics, crumpled up and thrown into the wastebasket. The new thing God wants to do in and through us usually will not conform to our initial expectations. We design; the Spirit of Jesus ultimately directs.

Most of us are wise to hold the structure details of our ministry plans loosely while we hold the deep values passionately and firmly. There will be many programming twists and turns as we travel on this planting road. Adaptive leadership requires that we "keep the main thing the main thing."

The life of Jesus—who he was and how he moved, engaged, messaged, served, saved, and challenged—is the new wine. Jesus would want us to be careful what we pour that expansive mixture into if we truly want to plant as he would.

Reflect: What assumptions or forms for ministry do you carry with you into your planting journey with Jesus? What designs might you need to hold loosely in order to fully engage the path Jesus has for you? How do you plan to "keep the main thing the main thing"?

Prayer: *Lord Jesus, you are the fresh wine that my community desperately needs. Help me to place no limits upon your Spirit. I release my ministry designs to you, holding them loosely, that I might follow you entirely. Amen.*

IT ALL STARTS WITH IDENTITY

Read Matthew 5:1-16.

> *"You are the salt of the earth. . . . You are the light of the world."*
>
> —Matthew 5:13-14

One of the confounding historical realities that sociologists and historians have wrestled to understand fully is the remarkable growth of the early church. Like a weed on steroids, the early Christian movement spread across the Roman world at a speed that nearly defies belief. From fewer than 10,000 believers at the end of the first century CE, the church likely numbered 6 million or more by 300 CE. However we may feel about the Roman emperor Constantine, who established Christianity as a state religion in 313 CE, his act does speak to the remarkable expansion that occurred in the years that followed.

Those early years and centuries of Christianity, however, were no cakewalk for disciples of Jesus. Their surrounding culture was pagan at every turn, with bizarre cults and sects that had far more adherents than Jesus ever did during his short ministry. In some remarkable ways, that culture was like ours, with great numbers of people who knew nothing of Christ or his kingdom. Nevertheless, the church grew rapidly, and so that era likely has something to teach us about kingdom expansion today.

Looking back so many centuries to reconstruct events cannot provide us with one-hundred-percent certainty in explaining all the reasons why such dramatic growth occurred. We could simply attribute it to a miracle

of God. At a human level, however, there are factors that can be measured. Gerald L. Sittser makes the case in his book *Resilient Faith: How
the Early Christian "Third Way" Changed the World* that the sense of identity in the early church was the major contributor to its unprecedented
vitality and growth.[1] That identity was rooted very deeply in how Jesus
named those early Christian followers as "salt of the earth" and "light of
the world." The identity that Jesus gave them was not that of an accommodating religion that adapted beliefs to fit their circumstances (which
would no longer be "salty"). Nor was their identity that of an isolationist,
privatized religion with weekend services but no evidence of belief the rest
of the week (and thus not illuminating). Their identity instead was a "third
way," says Sittser, one that was neither accommodating nor isolationist but
rather actively engaged with their world in faithful and winsome ways.
The identity that Jesus gave them was that of salt (an agent that cannot
be reduced to less than its essential saltiness) and light (a beam that cannot help but illuminate darkness). Salt and light must be actively engaged
in culture. We are "salt *of the earth*" and "light *of the world*." With these
remarks, Jesus is making a strong point about our self-awareness. From
that understanding flowed a community that was both faithful to Jesus
and engaging to outsiders. Consider the outcomes.

The early Christians demonstrated justice through racial, economic,
and gender reconciliation. The book of Acts gives us early pictures of that
economic and racial justice in Acts 2:44; 4:35; and 13:1-3. They showed
remarkable care for the poor, the weak, and the marginalized. Christians
were known in Rome to care for the impoverished and the sick, such that
by 350 CE, Emperor Julian, known for his efforts to revive paganism in
the city after Constantine, spoke openly of how Christianity advanced
because of the loving service it provided to those on society's fringe. There
is evidence of the early church's rescuing infants, through considerable
cost and efforts, who were subject to infanticide. (Those surviving children grew up to be passionate believers, for obvious reasons!) The early
Christians also demonstrated mutual respect in relationships with women
that previously had been characterized by oppression and abuse. They
were faithful to the example of Jesus and compelling in their local practices. They were salt and light.

Developing a new ministry must begin with a clear personal and corporate sense of identity that is deeply rooted in the gospel. Identity is where Jesus began, and identity is the wellspring from which all other efforts and plans pour forth. The entire Sermon on the Mount of Jesus in Matthew is a survey of identity markers for kingdom people and well worth a regular reading. That self-awareness that we are given in the kingdom is a rich and beautiful picture.

We are children of God. We are a new creation. We are a new humanity. We are redeemed. We are reconciled. We are blessed. We are called. We are sent. We are salt and light.

Reflect: How are you feeding your own soul and the souls of those you lead with the identity Jesus gives us? How does that identity speak to you deeply and directly about your call and purpose in mission? How can your community be salt and light in your mission field? In what ways should you resist accommodation to the culture around you while also not retreating from the world into a "holy huddle"?

Prayer: *Thank you, Lord Jesus, for my identity in you and in your cause. Thank you for naming me as salt and light. Help me to carry this identity with me today into each place I go and to each person I meet. Amen.*

✳ 23 ✳

VISIONING

Read Luke 9:51; Acts 16:6-10; Romans 15:20-29.

> *As the time approached for him to be taken up to heaven,*
> *Jesus resolutely set out for Jerusalem.*
>
> —Luke 9:51

Church planters are often asked about their vision statement, which might sound like just another business principle applied to Christian ministry. We are even asked to reduce it to an elevator speech so that it can be shared at a moment's notice. At first blush, this can sound simply like a promotional strategy. A closer look at Jesus and the early church, however, gives us several examples of a captivating vision and how that picture propelled the mission forward.

In Acts 16, Luke records an episode in the journeys of Paul where he comes to a crossroads in his mission work. Having made unsuccessful efforts to travel to the east, he receives a vision in the night to travel north and west into Macedonia. That Macedonian vision led Paul to plant churches in Philippi and Thessaloniki, and eventually it led him to Athens. Paul's general sense of mission, to advance the message of Jesus Christ (see Colossians 1:28-29), was increasingly focused upon a vision to reach Gentiles (see Acts 13:46-47; 18:6). He was, after all, uniquely gifted as a Jew from the Greek city of Tarsus who spoke the local language and who had open doors through which to travel by virtue of his Roman citizenship. Paul's Gentile-focused vision made perfect sense, given who he was. His vision flowed naturally from his identity and focused his efforts going forward.

Later in Paul's ministry, he talks about his vision to preach Christ where he has not been known as an evangelist and a church planter (see Romans 15:20) and then ultimately to go to Rome, and eventually on to Spain (see Romans 15:23-24). He makes a similar statement in 2 Corinthians 10:16, saying he wants to go to "the regions beyond" and not work in territory already evangelized. Paul's visioning is similar to that of Jesus, as he too had a general mission and calling "to do the will of him who sent me" (John 4:34), while at the same time he had a very specific vision to go to Jerusalem and offer his life up for the world ("Jesus resolutely set out for Jerusalem" [Luke 9:51]).

The mission of God, to go and make disciples of Jesus Christ for the transformation of the world, is a given for all who follow Jesus (see Matthew 28:18-20). The call to do our disciple-making work in the way Jesus would as servants of our Lord and of others is a universal calling for all those who claim to belong to Christ (see John 15:20). Our vision, however, is the unique way our gifts and passion come together in a specific time and a specific place for a specific people.

Brad is a friend who has struggled for many years with addiction. Over time, he hit rock bottom and experienced a transformation of his entire life. God used his journey and his weakness not only to move him into long-term spiritual recovery but also to give him a clear sense of calling and vision to plant a Jesus community in Minneapolis, his town, among those who have similar struggles. Brad has a clear picture of the recovery community he seeks to plant, largely because of his own spiritual awakening. So often, the vision God has for us comes when we look within our own lives and experiences for a signal. Other times, that vision for ministry comes from external promptings as we become aware of an underserved community. In either case, a vision for ministry involves a sense that God has uniquely brought us into a moment for a specific purpose. For Brad, the vision for a recovery congregation flows out of who he is in a deep and authentic way. People who know him see how it all comes together and can hear his passion.

Vision is sometimes referred to as a "preferred picture" of the future, but that language may be a bit tame. For most of us, our vision is a passion that propels us forward with inner drive. Vision does not dim when a few clouds roll in. Rather, vision looks deep into our heart and out onto our environment and "sees" what others may not yet imagine. It is a humble confidence in the power of Jesus to do something as yet unseen. Visioning is knowing and messaging our unique obedience to God and is therefore part of planting like Jesus.

Reflect: How has God planted a vision in your life and ministry? How are you making choices that help you move toward that vision? How are you messaging that in a compelling way to your closest partners and to your newest contacts?

Prayer: *God, I am grateful today for the experiences and circumstances of my life that give me a sense of direction and purpose. Speak to me through these and other means, that my vision for living and serving would be what you have for me in Jesus' name. Amen.*

— 24 —

EXTENDED FAMILY ON MISSION

Read Mark 3:20-35.

> "Whoever does God's will is my brother and sister and mother."

—Mark 3:35

Many of us were taught that pastors should maintain professional distance between themselves and others. More than healthy boundaries, we heard it as counsel not to form close relationships within the congregation we serve. While the notion of avoiding preferential relationships can make some sense sometimes, Jesus seems to work nearly 180 degrees in the other direction. Let's journey back to the earliest days of his work with fresh eyes, to see what could significantly change the way we do ministry today.

While Jesus was born and raised in Nazareth, he began and anchored much of his ministry in Capernaum. It was Capernaum where he called his first disciples, preached his first synagogue sermon, and healed many (see Mark 1:16-31). From there, Jesus ministered throughout the region, powerfully stirring so many people. This phase is often referred to as the Great Galilean ministry of Jesus. In his book *Family on Mission: Integrating Discipleship into Our Everyday Lives*, Mike Breen has called attention to something remarkable that takes place as Jesus transitions out of Nazareth. [1] Let's look at this closely.

In Mark 3, Jesus enters a home, and the crowds follow him, filling the space. This was likely a return to Capernaum and the home of Peter and Andrew, where he had been before. As Jesus begins teaching, he gets a word from someone who has noticed that his mother and brothers have followed him here out of concern. They actually think Jesus has gone a bit crazy, and they want to save him from himself and any further embarrassment to the family name (see v. 21). As Jesus' family members stand outside, trying to get to him, one of his followers inside mentions their presence to Jesus, expecting him to make special seating for them inside. Jesus however, knowing the skeptical attitude of his family, makes an astonishing statement: "Who are my mother and my brothers?" (v. 33). Then, looking at those seated in a circle around him inside, he says, "Here are my mother and my brothers! Whoever does God's will is my brother and sister and mother" (vv. 34-35). Jesus appears to be saying that at this point, the network of relationships around him is stronger than the bonds of his biological family. Here is a picture of Jesus, gathering people (the inner circle of the Twelve plus others) and forming a community together. We might call it part of his early church planting work. It is worth noting how deeply Jesus valued these relationships with fellow kingdom seekers. This was his family.

In the North American context, a typical household might be somewhere from two to four people. The affiliation often is blood relations (plus the family pets). In the time of Jesus, however, a household was *extended* family. And Jesus takes that extended family practice and extends it yet further. The affiliation he is forming is not about blood but rather about a common commitment to the kingdom of God. Whoever does the will of God is family.

John and Susan are spiritual pioneers who, every Sunday evening, opened their home for a community dinner with friends and neighbors. Each person brought something to the mix of soups, casseroles, and salads. After several months of formation and conversation, that group began to bond with a vision for creative community development. Together, they decided to start an urban garden, transform a neighborhood, and practice the principles of Christian community. The group grew, and John invited others he met from his contract work around town. Together, they saw relationships take root in their neighborhood and an expression of the kingdom come to be. The urban garden sprang up, and the group shared the joy of the produce with the community. John and Susan were forming an extended family on mission similar to the way Jesus did in Capernaum. Their simple practice not only created a wonderful community conversation among many new people but also demonstrated how close relationships from the start can bond people in a shared effort.

Rachel, who planted in a community of military families, remembers fondly the holidays when their church plant became "family" for those who had no extended family in town. Christmas, the Fourth of July, and birthdays all became occasions for being together on mission as they formed their new community of faith.

Jesus did not fit the mold for how religious professionals conduct themselves, and neither should we. *Being church* with your friends creates an affiliation that can build bonds as strong and, in many ways, as satisfying as family. This is how we plant like he did.

Reflect: How does Jesus' definition of family challenge you to think about ministry? How intentional are you at cultivating a sense of extended family on mission with those you are leading? What might you need to do to take that to a new level?

Prayer: *Jesus, I see how you drew people into community and helped them form bonds in your kingdom. Show me how I too can gather diverse people into a common experience with you, bringing transformation to our community, I pray. Amen.*

✳ 25 ✳

WHAT IS CHURCH?

Read Matthew 16:13-18; Acts 2:41-47.

> *"I will build my church, and the gates of Hades will not overcome it."*
>
> —Matthew 16:18

Reading the book of Acts as a church planter is a great way to "geek out" on our work when we feel the urge. Acts is church planting from cover to cover. Many of us, at some point in our planting journey, reflect upon this book as we struggle to "deconstruct church," remove all of the extraneous elements that get added (think buildings, budgets, programs, and a zillion meetings), and get back to the core essence of Christian community. Reading Acts can help peel away layers and give us keen insights. What is church after all of the unnecessary stuff is stripped away?

In Acts 2, we have a picture of the formation of the early church as a natural progression that was set in motion after a person professes faith in Christ, as Peter did in Matthew 16. That profession of faith, "You [Jesus] are the Messiah, the Son of the living God" (v. 16), sparks the beginning of discipleship. The presence of Jesus' disciples in proximity gives rise to a gathered group who seek to live out the kingdom life. In short, church is people coming together to practice living the kingdom life Jesus inaugurated in his ministry. A closer look at Acts 2 shows us this kingdom life in three basic dimensions.

First, it is immediately clear that the early church was about life *transformation*. The people wanted to hear from the apostolic witnesses who

had been with Jesus: "They devoted themselves to the apostles' teaching" (Acts 2:42). Imagine them pondering again the parables of Jesus or
the Sermon on the Mount or all that Jesus said about his mission at the
Last Supper. As they reflected upon the life and words of Jesus, they
were going deep into dimensions of personal and corporate transformation. The gospel changes everything, and we can read in the epistles how
Paul and others sought to draw out the message of Jesus and its many
implications (see 1 Corinthians 11:23 and following; 1 Corinthians 15:3
and following).

Second, it is evident that the early church was about genuine *relationships*. The followers shared and cared for one another, meeting together
in public places and in their homes: "Every day they continued to meet
together in the temple courts. They broke bread in their homes and ate
together with glad and sincere hearts" (Acts 2:46). Imagine the lifetime
relationships that were formed as these believers discovered together the
joys and the challenges of following Jesus. The way the gospel formed a
sense of genuine family was often indicated by the phrase "one another,"
used by early writers (nearly one hundred times in the New Testament[1])
as a tie to Jesus, who called them to "love one another" (John 13:34).

Third, there is a direct reference to service and *mission* to those in
need: "They sold property and possessions to give to anyone who had
need" (Acts 2:45). Like ours, theirs was a society with many human needs.
Into that predicament they came, with spiritual and physical healing. As a
result, they saw miracles that brought joy and blessing. Imagine a culture
that did not have the social services we might tend to depend upon. It was
the followers of Jesus who were led to close the gap between suffering and
hope. They made it their business to give and serve freely, as Jesus had
(see Romans 12:9 and following).

A church planter friend of mine used to take the month of January
every year to preach those three simple defining features of church—
transformation, relationships, and mission. He would make a passionate
appeal for people not to make church more complicated than these simple
things. On one particular occasion, the congregation held worship in a
shopping mall courtyard to make the point that church is not a place.

Church certainly involves many activities, including the sacraments; leadership development; music and the arts in worship; outreach to those near and far; and, of course, way too many meetings. However, most of the descriptions we find in the New Testament fit under those three main headings of life transformation, genuine relationships, and service to others. The early church did not come up with this formula on their own. They saw it clearly in the example of Jesus himself, who lived these simple values authentically over time with revolutionary results. We do well when we keep our objectives straightforward and plant like Jesus.

Reflect: How does the message found in Acts 2 help you think about church planting work and your priorities? How can it help you communicate your mission to others? How can you keep your ministry simple?

Prayer: *Lord of the church, I place this ministry of planting before you as yours. This is your church, not mine. It is your church by virtue of your lordship and by virtue of your design. Help me to be faithful to you and your purposes as the head of the church. I pray, in your name. Amen.*

✻ 26 ✻

WHY SMALL GROUPS?

Read John 13:34-35; Romans 15:1-7.

> "A new command I give you: Love one another. As I have
> loved you, so you must love one another. By this everyone
> will know that you are my disciples, if you love one another."
>
> —John 13:34-35

One of the essential building blocks of a new faith community is the small group. Grow a network of small groups, so the theory goes, and you have the necessary base to launch public worship. This may be true, but the reason for small groups goes beyond their serving as stepping stones to a grand-opening worship day. In his book *Sticky Church*, Larry Osborne memorably names the connecting effect small groups can have on people. Groups become the "sticky" factor as relationships flourish and function like glue. It's a kind of organizational and sociological way of thinking about the importance of small groups.[1] This is all good and true, but the reason for small groups actually goes even deeper.

Romans 15 is a snapshot of relational, small-group ministry. Considering that the audience for this book of Romans included people in a house church (see 16:5), it is worth seeing the chapter through that lens. This is likely a close-knit community. Paul tells his readers to "accept one another" (v. 7), and he anchors it in the practice of Jesus, saying that we should "live in harmony with one another, in accordance with Christ Jesus" (v. 5, NRSV). The way of Jesus is about relationships that are deep and rich. To fully appreciate that quality, consider the reciprocal pronoun "one another." It is a key phrase that traces back to Jesus—"A new command I give you: Love one another" (John 13:34). "One another" sources back to Jesus. Jesus promoted reciprocal, loving relationships with the Twelve (see John 13:35); and the importance of mutual love blossomed in the writings of Paul, Peter, and James.

The Greek word *allélón* ("al-lay'-lone"), from which we get the phrase "one another," occurs ninety-seven times in the New Testament.[2] It is found mostly in the Epistles but also in the Gospels. Sometimes it is used to promote unity ("be at peace with one another"; "forgive one another"; "bear with one another"; "do not grumble with one another"). Sometimes it is used to promote humility ("serve one another"; "give preference to one another"). Sometimes it is used to promote care ("be devoted to one another"; "bear one another's burdens;" "provoke one another to love and good deeds"). Again, all of these can ultimately be traced back to Jesus, who said, "A new command I give you: Love one another. As I have loved you, so you must love one another. By this everyone will know that you are my disciples, if you love one another" (John 13:34-35). The command from Jesus to love, when worked out in relationships, gives us nearly one hundred examples in the Bible to chew on. This is what sticky Christian community looks like!

Small groups can be thought of as a passing trend that is a "take-it-or-leave-it" type of option. If, however, we see them as the optimal environment in which to live out the values of Christian community and disciple making, then it looks otherwise. If you think about it, it would be fairly difficult to live the "one another" values of the New Testament exclusively with one hundred or more people seated in tidy rows for an hour on weekends. It would be much more likely in a group of five or fifteen where there are shared meals and experiences and the give and take around applying faith to life. Little wonder that the early church established a rhythm of both large- and small-group gatherings (see Acts 5:42).

Some time back, I was invited to join a men's group where we enjoyed a schedule of activities together. I always looked forward to our next event, whether it was an evening grilling dinner and pitching horseshoes or a morning out on a lake, fishing. Over time, that group began to build trust, and our conversations went deeper. We would meet for breakfast every other Saturday and would informally "check in" after a round of pancakes. One guy would have had a frustrating week with his job, while another would be celebrating a personal success in single-parenting his teenager. Around the circle, the conversation was shared with intent listening and encouraging words. Christian community began to show up, and the group became a high point in the week.

That experience reminded me again that "small group" is more than a description of organizational structure. It is also more than a passing trend. Small groups are Christian community the way Jesus intended. Small-group development is a part of planting like Jesus.

Reflect: What value do you place upon small-group formation and development? How effective are you at developing healthy group practices? What might you need to do to develop stronger relationships through groups?

Prayer: *God, as you exist in a small community of Father, Son, and Spirit, help me grow small communities of your Spirit where people can practice and experience the love of Jesus. Help us form relationships where the life of Christ will be lived out. I pray, in Jesus' name. Amen.*

✸ 27 ✸

THE WISDOM OF TEAMS

Read Mark 3:14-19; Acts 13:42–14:3.

> [Jesus] appointed twelve that they might be with him and
> that he might send them out to preach.
>
> —Mark 3:14

Ministry can be lonely. Planting pioneers do not walk into an office on day one with a staff and office parties. Some of us, if we are solo "parachute planters," may not even have a welcoming committee on our first day. Little wonder that Mark 3:14 profoundly states that Jesus recruited the Twelve—first, "that they might be with him" in relationship as partners; and second, to accomplish a task where "he might send them out to preach"; Jesus needed a team. In that simple group formation, Jesus foresaw the awareness we share today of the potential that teams have in business, industry, and many other areas to elevate performance.[1] Teamwork is good for us, as it is good for accomplishing the mission God has given us to do. Jesus has set us an example.

Paul was also a team builder. Over the years of his work, he teamed up with Silas, Barnabas, Luke, Timothy, Titus, Priscilla, and Aquila for regional work, and he also worked with many other local partners, including Erastus, Gaius, Aristarchus, Tychicus, and Trophimus. Far from being a lone ranger, as he sometimes appears to be, Paul knew that his pioneer planting work would require strong partnerships if he was going to succeed, and he gave thanks for those bonds (see Philippians 1:3-5). Let's look closely at an example of how Paul benefited from a team approach.

In Acts 13–14, Paul and Barnabas are teamed up, having been sent
out together from the church in Antioch to extend the Gentile mission
into new territory (see Acts 13:2). It is a remarkable series of events, as
the church, which in the past had grown amidst persecution scatterings,
is now undertaking the first proactive effort to extend the mission. This
first team effort made a significant impact, with entire cities and regions
hearing the kingdom news (see Acts 13:44, 49). The team also faced considerable opposition (see Acts 14:2-5), and we might imagine the courage
they had together that might have wavered, had Paul been alone. They
were so effective together (see them team-preaching and -teaching in Acts
14:1) that they were able to reach into Jewish and Greek circles with mea-
surable results. Imagine their team meetings as they worked together to
navigate the opportunity and challenge of their circumstances. As the
temperature rose with opposition, they remained bold together (see Acts
13:46) and showed resilience when they faced opposition (see Acts 13:51-
52; 14:5-7).

Most of us plant solo; Nate and Keith planted together. They knew
one another and were aware of the way their individual styles worked
together. With that keen self-awareness, they formed a planting team and
experienced success. For many of the rest of us, we will need to form
partnerships and teams along the way, while we may still remain the solo
point leader. Teams do not require everyone to be in equal roles. They
do, however, require some essential qualities in the members, including
patience in decision-making; willingness to be open to other perspectives;
investment in building trust; and, above all, good communication. For
Nate and Keith, the benefits made all the difference. One of those benefits was the impact their relationship had upon other ministry leaders in
their plant, who saw how a team functioned and carried that approach
over into their ministry teams. The whole project grew stronger.

Being a team is different from being a work group. Think of it as the
difference between being in a golf league and being on a basketball team.
In one, the accent is on the individual performance; while with the other,
the emphasis is on the performance of the group. Teams rely more upon
group ownership, discussion, discernment, and cooperative decision-
making. Teams call for complementary skills and group accountability. It

is that collective and interactive commitment that gives a true team the edge over a work group where people remain in their individual work silos.

The list of teaming benefits from the story of Paul and Barnabas is significant. The two of them had a greater impact together. They had greater boldness together. They had more resilience together. In so many ways, they were better together. Many of us feel that team formation and development will slow us down. It is true that teamwork takes time. It will require more meetings and more patience. However, Paul and Barnabas, Nate and Keith, Jesus and the Twelve—they show us the wisdom of teams.

If we want to go fast, we go solo. If we want to go far, we go with a team. In so doing, we plant like Jesus.

Reflect: How are you doing at modeling and building ministry teams? Where in your planting work should you be forming a team rather than going solo? What team practices must you develop to maximize this essential practice?

Prayer: *Jesus, I recognize you do not expect me to do this kingdom work alone. Your life in ministry points me to the importance of building a team to impact my mission field. As I seek to grow leaders in my context, I pray you will deepen relationships and develop our sense of unity as we carry out the work you are guiding us into. Amen.*

❊ 28 ❊

ASKING FOR COMMITMENT

Read Luke 14:15-35.

> *"Suppose one of you wants to build a tower. Won't you first sit down and estimate the cost to see if you have enough money to complete it?"*
>
> —Luke 14:28

Ask any church planter, and most would agree: At some point in the process, you need committed people. The "we-will-take-anybody" phase sooner or later gives way to a clear understanding that without people who will deeply commit their time, talent, and treasure to a new faith community, the future is pretty bleak. Asking for commitment is not always easy. We often get that "ask" tangled up with our own need for approval or security or success. Throw in some rejection experienced from your childhood, and asking people to commit to a new church can push our anxiety upward. Again, our Lord has helpful wisdom.

When Jesus pioneered the kingdom, he asked people to commit to a new way of life. His "Come, follow me" (Mark 1:17) eventually led to stories and direct teaching about commitment. In Luke 14, large crowds are following Jesus, and he delivers a high-commitment message that most of us would have expected to land like a lead balloon. For example, he says, "Ditch your family if you really want to follow me" (Luke 14:26, paraphrased). But Jesus often uses hyperbole to make a point, and the verses that follow explain his powerful opening line (see Luke 14:28-33). In short, Jesus wants the crowds to count the cost before they go much farther in their journey with him. Counting the cost is about measuring the personal impact this will have on our lives. It is about taking commitment seriously. Let's look closer at how Jesus communicated.

First, Jesus did not call for commitment before having built relationship. The crowds that followed Jesus in Luke 14 had done so for a time. They were likely among the multitude of the five thousand who had been fed with a few loaves and fish. They were also likely aware of, if not present at, one or more of Jesus' remarkable healings or his unforgettable teaching on the mountainside. Commitment was not a hit-and-run conversation. People need time to check you out and see that your leadership is worth their following. The commitment conversation likely does not come until there has been time given to establishing an authentic relationship.

Second, note that Jesus asked them to commit first *to him* before he asked them to commit to a project. For him, it was ultimately about the followers being "my disciples." Engaging people in various efforts along the way is well and good. But when it comes to pitching real commitment, the idea is for people to make their commitment with Jesus primary and their commitment with the ministry secondary. Commitment is first about growing as a disciple and secondarily about helping to start a new church.

Third, notice that Jesus wanted them to "sit down and consider" (v. 31). There was no pressure there, only the request to think things over and make their decision after giving this some honest, personal reflection.

A planter friend of mine designed a tool to help interested people "Sit Down and Consider" a commitment to their start-up effort, a partnership document that outlined four boxes or blanks for an individual to check: _____ I will commit to pray; _____ I will commit my time; _____ I will commit my talent; _____ I will commit my treasure. Below each heading, there were smaller boxes to check for the amount of time committed (attending worship, participating in small groups, praying, and so on), specific talents (including a listing of volunteer areas where volunteers were needed), and the amount of treasure pledged (commitment to a monthly financial contribution). This partnership form was posted on a webpage where the planter could direct people who were interested and where the planter would be able to use their responses for reflection—and, later, in initiating commitment conversations with those who had responded. Helping new people commit requires providing a process whereby they can count the cost in that decision.

Finally, we never go wrong by asking people first to pray about a commitment. Our real desire is for them to develop their connection to Jesus, not just to our project. That overarching priority in the process of commitment sends the message that a commitment conversation is ultimately not about us and our start-up project. It is really about prompting the people we encounter to always be considering taking fresh, new steps with Jesus.

Reflect: What is your process for asking people to commit? How does the pattern Jesus used help you think about this vital step? What might you need to change in order to be most effective in asking for commitments?

Prayer: *Lord, as you called people to yourself first and then into your mission, help me to clearly do the same. Give me wisdom and boldness in asking people to "count the cost" of being a disciple. I pray, in your name. Amen.*

❧ 29 ❧

DIVERSITY AND ALIGNMENT

Read John 17:1-26; Acts 13:1-3.

> *"My prayer is not for them alone. I pray also for those who will believe in me through their message, that all of them may be one, Father, just as you are in me and I am in you. May they also be in us so that the world may believe that you have sent me."*
>
> —John 17:20-21

The mission field in North America is becoming diverse at a remarkable rate. The US Census Bureau projects that relatively soon, Caucasians will no longer be the majority group in the United States.[1] Wise planters are working where they can to build diversity into their leadership teams in response to a changing culture and out of a deeper commitment to kingdom values. Similarly, immigrant planters coming to North America have often focused on first-generation immigrants initially, only to shift later toward a multicultural vision, as a second generation with diverse values and language preferences grows up in the congregation. This accelerating trend in North America turns our eyes in a fresh way back to the diverse roots of the Christian movement in the book of Acts.

A tipping point in the early Christian movement is found in Acts 13 and the picture of the church at Antioch. Prior to this, the focus of the mission had been around Jewish individuals, such as Peter and Stephen. By Acts 11, however, the scattering effect of persecution had landed some in Antioch, where they encountered Greek speakers who were receptive to their message. The result was a surge in growth and the establishment of the Antioch church.

The makeup of the Antioch church is worth a close look. First, we can assume some were Jewish as a remnant of the original mission group, including Barnabas and Saul. Acts 13 adds that there were those (including Lucius) from Cyrene, which was a city in northern Africa. In addition, Luke acknowledges people from Cyprus, the Mediterranean island (see Acts 11:20) and Manaen, who had been raised among the aristocratic household of Herod. Immediately, we see social, economic, racial, and cultural diversity in this early congregation. They all seemed to come together around the gospel and speaking Greek. (Beyond that common ground, they must have had very interesting conversations and eclectic potluck suppers!)

Diversity is a beautiful thing, and we celebrate those congregations that are seeking to look like the community around them. It is encouraging to see that in America today, there is a significant trend among congregations to embrace diversity as a core value and to engage the deep change that is required to live it. Clear voices are emerging to lead the way.[2] There is, however, another picture from Antioch that we should not miss. Acts 13:2-3 describes how this diverse group was united in mission, setting aside Paul and Barnabas and sending them off together. Picture all these various constituent groups agreeing on pooling their resources to focus on one missionary project. Imagine the conversations that had to take place so they could all join in a common sense of mission. They were aligned in a shared cause.

In some ways, we might say that alignment is tougher to develop than diversity. Diversity is something we celebrate as the world becomes smaller and our demographics change. Alignment runs contrary to our nature, as we tend toward focusing upon our personal identity and rights. Many will come to our start-up efforts with an agenda or think of themselves as representing a constituency. Alignment requires trust, mutuality, respect, submission, listening, compromise, agreement, and hearts attuned first to the mission of God above all. In church planting, the alignment that we experience in the early years cannot be assumed going forward. We must continue to work for it and lift it up.

Jesus saw this need for alignment in his future mission, when he prayed that his followers would be one (see John 17:20-21). How much farther and faster would his mission advance if a mosaic of people could agree together like they did in Antioch? Diversity and alignment, together in mission, capture the very heart and prayer of our Lord Jesus. This is what planting like Jesus looks like.

Reflect: How are you doing at developing diverse leadership in your work? How are you doing at uniting that diverse people into a common purpose? What might you need to do to move forward in diversity and alignment?

Prayer: *Lord of all creation, I thank you for your vision to bring all peoples into your kingdom. Help me experience the beautiful mosaic you have for us and empower me to align people together in your mission, for Jesus' sake. Amen.*

❊ 30 ❊

RECRUITING VOLUNTEERS

Read Mark 1:16-20.

> *As Jesus walked beside the Sea of Galilee, he saw Simon
> and his brother Andrew casting a net into the lake, for they
> were fishermen. "Come, follow me," Jesus said, "and I will
> send you out to fish for people."*
>
> —Mark 1:16-17

Start-up ventures such as church planting are heavily volunteer-dependent. We cannot do this without donated hours and talent. Scan the internet, and you can find plenty of advice on how to recruit volunteer leaders—recommendations such as, "Never pressure anyone into volunteer leadership"; "Always clarify expectations"; "Make sure leaders have the authority to get their responsibilities done." All good stuff. Jesus models a foundational principle, however, that can make all the difference in start-up work. Let's consider again his example for us.

Mark 1:16-20 is a simple story of Jesus calling his first disciples that we might tend to pass over quickly. Note, however, that Jesus does not put out a sign-up sheet to see who is open to following him; this actually would have been more like the practice of rabbis in Jesus' day, where the student would pursue the rabbi to become the rabbi's disciple. Jesus, by contrast, takes the initiative and pursues the people he wants to be part of his team. Simon, Andrew, James, and John receive a personal invitation from Jesus to get on board the kingdom train. Later on, Jesus will personally invite others. Ask anyone who has recruited great volunteers successfully, and you likely will discover that the best people will respond only if you personally ask them; it is almost always true. But there is more here to observe.

It is likely that the disciples had had some prior experience with Jesus before that day he met them and called them to follow. Commentators suggest that they may have had as much as a year's or more exposure to his miracles and teaching before this pivotal moment. That said, Mark indicates that Simon and Andrew did not drag their feet when they were asked: "At once they left their nets and followed him" (Mark 1:18). When Jesus came to James and John, it seems their response was similar, as "they left their father Zebedee in the boat" and followed (Mark 1:20). Imagine these early disciples walking away from the family business, into the unknown. What they lacked in spiritual maturity they made up for in readiness to follow, and therein lies insight for us.

Secular leadership training has coined the phrase "Hire for attitude, train for skill." It is a simple prescription that puts the accent upon the inner motivation of potential employees or volunteers before we expect them to have all the abilities needed for the roles in which we imagine them. I saw this once when Kelly, a communications leader, recruited Paula to take over a key volunteer tech role. Kelly knew that there were others actually more qualified for the position but who were not reliable and were a bit resistant to being trained; she had detected within them a "coachability deficit" that gave her pause. Paula's faithfulness in the roles she had played earlier demonstrated her stellar attitude and willingness to be coached. That character quality made all the difference over the long haul.

So often, when we recruit for leadership, we look for ability: "If we had that skill set on our team, then we would quickly be able to plug them into a role and move on to what is next." However, this does not seem to be the way Jesus worked. Jesus appears to look first for availability and attitude. Granted, this approach can be slower on the front end; it can take us more time to develop those persons to their potential. We will need to meet with them regularly, coach them in more detail, and invest in some training for them. But in the long run, we are likely to cultivate the best leaders when we start with attitude.

It has been said, "There is a short path that takes longer, and there is a longer path that is shorter." Jesus seemed to choose a longer path when he selected his average disciples; but over time and with his training, they proved to be the right leaders. We are wise to follow his example.

Reflect: Whom might you know who has shown willingness but may have been passed over because they are not skilled enough to lead? For whom do you need to stop waiting and simply ask them directly to step up in their discipleship or leadership? What will you need to do to support them and help them succeed?

Prayer: *Lord, give me eyes to see the potential, skills, and gifts in people committed to this church plant. As our leadership considers needs of the ministry and identifies roles for volunteers, help us discern where your Spirit is leading. Jesus, give us courage to ask and faith to believe that you will continue to call people to your kingdom work. Amen.*

✦ 31 ✦

PEOPLE DEVELOPMENT

Read Luke 22:15; John 13-17.

"I have eagerly desired to eat this Passover with you."

—Luke 22:15

If I just had a few people who weren't so flaky, maybe we could actually get the traction we need to get somewhere!" It's a common sentiment in volunteer-intensive start-up work. We all need that reliable volunteer who has amazing experience, strong people skills, free evenings and weekends, a generous pocketbook, and a willingness to jump in and help where needed. The day it dawns upon us that this person will never show up can be pretty crushing. Thankfully, we are not the first people to face this struggle.

Jesus started his ministry with very common laborers. It's worth stating that he did not begin his work with the Twelve by recruiting them into a grand church-planting strategy in which he needed to fill some programmatic positions. He did not start with an organizational design and then "plug recruits into it." Jesus just started with them. Only them. Twelve average people. The development of the disciples was the first program Jesus led. As Reggie McNeal reminds us in his book *Missional Renaissance: Changing the Scorecard for the Church*, people development matters more than program development.[1] Most of us will not escape this basic reality in our pioneer planting.

In Luke 22:15, Jesus takes that development of his closest followers to a pivotal point as he expresses his deep desire to be with his disciples for

Passover. For several years now, he has walked with them, showing them and teaching them the principles of the kingdom. Now, it is time for his last meal with them. This evening, he will teach them at length about servant leadership; the coming Holy Spirit; their relationship as vine and branches; his desire for their unity; and, above all, his great passion for them soon to be fully revealed (see John 13–17). It is remarkable how much of our recorded teaching from Jesus occurs on this night alone.

It would also be a mistake to assume that their marathon meeting in the upper room was the preferred way Jesus developed his disciples. Leading up to this night, they have had a remarkable range of experiences together, including travels throughout Galilee and Judea and ministry to crowds and individuals, along with encounters with adversaries and the evil one. They have seen storms at sea, and they have seen stories from Jesus hold the attention of skeptics. They have seen outcast Samaritans flock to Jesus, and they have seen followers desert him. Most of the spiritual formation that took place in the lives of Peter, James, John, and the rest of the Twelve took place in real-time ministry. Because they had done significant time "in the field," they were probably like sponges when Jesus taught them that night. So, it was as if he were pouring all he could into them in one last evening of instruction. He understood that if he could form them as individuals and as leaders, the kingdom initiative that would emerge in subsequent months and years would flow powerfully. Imagine Jesus, pacing his way through that night, moving from lesson to lesson. See him leaning into the conversation, connecting deeply with his disciples as individuals and as a small group. Listen to him as he responds to their questions and hopes for the future.

Chris is a planter friend who has done a great job "growing people up." One of his practices is to develop individuals and leaders by coaching them. Meeting once per month, he helps them take ownership of their goals, set priorities, identify challenges, and (perhaps most critically) become accountable for their action steps. It is this regular monthly meeting and investment that shifts the focus from just managing life to developing individuals to their potential. In this practice, Chris is leading as Jesus did when he gave so much of his time and attention in the development of his disciples.

Jesus developed people at different levels. He engaged multitudes, large groups (see the seventy-two in Luke 10:1-23), a small group of twelve, and an inner circle of three (see Mark 14:32-34). Yet he never lost sight of the individual. Each one is a custom job. Each comes with a unique history, particular hopes, and a unique set of gifts. Some will develop through study. Most will require experience and the personal growth that comes through reflection and accountability. Walking with people through their development is an essential part of planting like Jesus.

Reflect: Would you say your energy is directed mostly toward program development or people development? What do you need to do to prioritize people development? Whom should you be coaching on a monthly basis?

Prayer: *God, I can be tempted to rush to the programming while failing to develop individuals. Help me to see the potential in each person and fully partner with your Spirit in the development of people for your mission. Amen.*

✦ 32 ✦

GIVING AWAY AUTHORITY

Read Matthew 10:1-6; 28:18-20.

Jesus called his twelve disciples to him and gave them authority to drive out impure spirits and to heal every disease and sickness.

—Matthew 10:1

It is a bit arresting how quickly Jesus sends his neophyte disciples out with authority. In Matthew 10, they are still "wet behind the ears" and "wobbly in their legs" when Jesus sends them out with authority to lead in ways that, by most any standard, would be considered bold and audacious. Watch how he gives them authority over spiritual forces such as unclean spirits and every kind of disease. It's like he is issuing them a license to practice healing medicine before they have barely begun medical school!

As planting leaders, this sounds risky, given that we work with people who may be inexperienced and untested in ministry. When should we release them to lead a small group or head up a ministry team? Should we follow Jesus' lead and anoint those who show up and are willing, though they may still be far from mature? What if they do something terrible, like teaching heresy?

The Gospels are full of examples of Jesus sending out unqualified people to do his work. First, he sends out the Twelve after a fairly brief time with them, giving them authority to demonstrate the power of the kingdom (see Mark 3:14-15; 6:7). This release of authority comes before another commissioning of seventy-two disciples to do similar kingdom work, as recorded in Luke 10. In John 14:12, Jesus pumps up the confidence of his future followers, saying they will do "greater things" than he did himself. Stop and think about it: Are we really qualified for that endorsement?! Elsewhere, Jesus tells Peter—far from a model for spiritual maturity—that he has authority to "bind" and "loose" and to "forbid" or "permit," which seems like a lot of trust to put in a flaky fisherman (see Matthew 16:19; 18:18, NLT). Then, in Matthew 28, Jesus, claiming all authority in himself, sends his disciples to do the work of his mission—teaching and baptizing—claiming that he and his authority are with them until the "end of the age" (v. 20). To summarize, the Lord of history comes into the world for a relatively short time and completes his mission within a few years, during which he routinely releases others with full permission to represent his purposes. Then, while the kingdom movement is as fragile as a newborn baby, he leaves the whole effort to rookies, saying he will return to see their progress. None of this sounds like how I would do it.

Carrie is a small-group leader in a new church. She had no idea that her pastor considered her leadership of a group to be a grooming ground for weekend preaching. When the time came to ask her about this possibility, she certainly did not feel she was ready. But Carrie had learned how to study the Bible and how to lead a group discipleship conversation. She had experienced how the words of Jesus get under your skin when you live them and then how your heart bursts with a message to share. She was not ready to be a regular preacher, by any means, but she was ready to speak publicly; and when she did, people deeply connected with her message. That experience opened a new arena for Carrie, who has grown into new opportunities. Her story says much about Carrie and much more about her pastor, who believed in her gifts and did not feel threatened by the emergence of another effective teacher in the church.

Reflect upon Jesus and his empowering style further. Notice how he shares with them deep insights into his ministry so that they felt they were on the inside track with him. See how he allows them to succeed and fail in a context of grace and truth. Watch how he gives them the clear framework of his kingdom purposes within which to work. Catch how he has confidence in them, probably before they have full confidence in themselves. Observe how he follows up with them to process their experiences and learning in the field.

Empowering people with authority to lead takes many different forms. At its core, however, it requires that leaders are secure in their own gifts, such that we can happily see others step up and succeed. It often requires that we help individuals who are a bit insecure to see their potential and then that we stay close by, to coach them through trial and error. It most always requires that we see our best work to be when we are not the only person with the gifts and responsibility who gets the job done. Rather, we must come to see ourselves as the person with the capacity to develop others to their potential and then release them, like Jesus did, with authority.

This practice of seeing potential in others, training, coaching, and giving away authority is part of planting like Jesus.

Reflect: How intentional are you at releasing people with authority to lead in ministry? What may be holding you back? Whom might you need to equip and release in the coming days?

Prayer: *Lord Jesus, as you equipped, empowered, and sent your disciples in mission, help me to do the same. Grow me in your generative Spirit, as you saw the potential within individuals and drew that out of them for their good, for the good of others, and for your glory, I pray. Amen.*

✳ 33 ✳

ORGANIZING FOR MINISTRY

Read John 16:12-15; 1 Corinthians 12:1-13.

> *"[The Spirit of truth] will glorify me because it is from me that he will receive what he will make known to you."*
>
> —John 16:14

There is no one way to structure a community of people dedicated to the mission of Jesus. There is no one way to design a church. You have probably seen enough variety to affirm that reality. In some parts of the world, the most common structure is a network of house assemblies. Many congregations in North America are smaller-sized groups led by volunteers and a bivocational or covocational pastor. Still others are large congregations with specialized staff teams and dozens of small groups. How you organize a church can depend upon where you worship, how you measure growth, where authority is found, how people network, or how you do mission. There are so many options and there is so much room for Spirit-led creativity.

I have recently been inspired by congregations emerging in workplace settings where employees shape the mission and identity of their ministry around a common corporate setting. Imagine showing up at your cubicle knowing that on your lunch break, you would be huddling with your faith community for Bible study. I love the emerging "dinner churches" that are popping up for the sake of reaching new people. Imagine that, church organized around food; what's not to like! The genius of Jesus is evident, as he did not overly prescribe a specific structure for his body, the church.

He designed his kingdom to be organizationally adaptive, an ideal quality when growth is a key objective.

When Jesus looked to the future with his disciples, he did, however, talk about the work of his Spirit that would flow through his followers (see John 16:12-15). This reality would set seeds in the soil for ministry order. That Spirit of Christ was seen by Paul to have gifted the early church for ministry (see Ephesians 4:11-13; 1 Corinthians 12:1 and following). It is that Spirit that would gift them such that they could be the very presence of Christ as his body in the world. So, as church planters, how might this help us think about organizing for ministry? A few things are worth considering.

First, everyone has a role to play in the church as Jesus envisioned it. His Spirit would fill every one of his followers, such that each could make a contribution. No one is to sit by and just passively observe, month after month. Church was never designed to promote spectators. As the early church reflected upon that filling of the Spirit, they believed that the roles to be played are fundamentally about serving in love. (Note that 1 Corinthians 13, defining the qualities of love, is in the middle of Paul's teaching on gifts of the Spirit.) Those acts of service can be done for the sake of those in the community of faith (teachers or leaders, for example) or for the sake of those outside the community of faith (apostolic missionaries or evangelists). Some gifts seem to cluster, such as gifts of "giving" or "administration" or "helping," which may serve a bit more behind the scenes; while the "teacher," "prophet," and "shepherd" are more visible. Each area of service is needed, and together they begin to create a culture and structure for service.

Bruce L. Bugbee, author of *Network: The Right People, in the Right Places, for the Right Reasons, at the Right Time*,[1] has worked for years to promote the biblical principle of empowering people with their gifts in ministry. It is a principle that is especially important in planting work. Early on, when we take the time to help people discern where they naturally fit using a spiritual gifts inventory and then equip them in that area, we unleash God-given potential. We not only help individuals gain clarity on how to serve but also set the stage for teams to form around areas of ministry, including care, leadership, outreach, social justice, and evangelism. The gifts of the Spirit of Jesus begin to provide a path for ministry organization.

In summary, we could say that Jesus did not prescribe a particular type of structure for the early church. He designed kingdom communities to be adaptive. Jesus did, however, prescribe a source of empowerment (his Spirit) that would be distributed in different ways to people who would exercise gifts with different areas of responsibility. Those areas of responsibility, along with the realities of our cultural and physical context, can help us discern a structure for ministry that reflects the body of Christ. This is good news.

Reflect: How are you discovering the gifts of the Spirit among your people? What are the next steps for you as you mobilize those people for ministry? How is that leading you in your organizing for ministry?

Prayer: *Thank you, God, for the gifts you have given those who have gathered with me in this planting effort. Reveal the order you have for our ministry together, such that all gifts are fully released for your work. I pray in Jesus' name. Amen.*

❈ 34 ❈

MEMBERS AND PARTNERS

Read Luke 9:24; 1 Corinthians 12:12-27; Philippians 1:3-6.

> *"Whoever wants to save their life will lose it, but whoever loses their life for me will save it."*
>
> —Luke 9:24

Most of us would probably have to confess that we are conditioned to be consumers and that we so easily think and behave like consumers. We learn to be on the lookout for the next "best deal" and to hang on to our receipts "just in case." Consumerism is so prevalent today that the invitation to make a commitment to a church can land a bit flat: *What if something better comes along?* It is a challenging reality that consumerism runs through the veins of those we seek to reach.

Jesus, by contrast, leads a countercultural kingdom where losing ourselves to a greater purpose unlocks abundant life (see Luke 9:24). Church planter Paul uses two images in the New Testament that build out the contrast. In Philippians 1:3-6, Paul gives thanks for his "[partners] in the gospel" in Philippi (v. 5). We know that those early partners in Philippi went on to become the early participants in the new church plant there. In 1 Corinthians 12, Paul uses the metaphor of the church being a body with many parts or "members." Partners and members are different from consumers. They are committed through thick and thin.

Some simply reject the idea of membership as a business or organizational notion that is unbiblical. It is true that membership, when it is thought to be like membership in a club, would have been foreign to Paul.

That sort of membership is about privilege and status, and it contributes to a consumer mentality. But the early church's pattern was more about partnership than privilege, and Paul's use of the word *members* points primarily toward mutual responsibility: "For just as the body is one and has many members, and all the members of the body, though many, are one body, so it is with Christ. . . . Now you are the body of Christ and individually members of it (1 Cor. 12:12, 27, NRSV). Immediately after this, the writer identifies gifted people whom God has appointed to serve. Membership is not about privilege; it is about being a contributing partner: "And God has appointed in the church first apostles" (v. 28, NRSV).

Rob is a planter friend who took this notion of partnership seriously and developed a dramatic yearly event to make his point. Each year, he would wipe out the membership list of the church to zero on a weekend and in that same weekend service ask people who wanted to become partners to "recommit" to the responsibility of being an active part of the body of Christ. Each year, people had to reconsider their relationship with the ministry; coasting along as a member with privileges was not an option. Longtime "churchy" people were rather unsettled by the thought, while new folks received it as a great idea.

Perhaps Rob's strategy for helping people think biblically about membership is worth considering. Ultimately, our goal is to help people fully participate in the body of Christ, all doing their part. Another friend and planter, Whitney, chose a creative way of making a similar point with new joiners. She hosted a collaborative cooking event where new joiners worked together to make a common meal. That experience spoke volumes to participants about the kind of hands-on relationship she wanted with each of them in the ministry. It also created a great environment to form new friendships.

With membership at a resort or in a club, we tend to think of paying someone else to do the tasks that make for a pleasant environment. But this is not a helpful frame of mind in ministry. So, while Paul uses the word *member* in 1 Corinthians 12, we are wise to explain that term in the context of the "parts" of the body and the "partnership in the gospel" of Philippians 1:5. In a church, everyone has a gift and a responsibility to use that gift to further the mission. No position is superior, and no position is unnecessary. All are needed and valued. Partners are to use their gifts in a spirit of love toward the wider community. Partners work toward unity in the mission. Partnership is what members do for the sake of one shared kingdom cause.

Jesus invited people to commit to him as Lord and Savior (see John 14:6; Matthew 11:28-30). *Partnership* and *membership* are words that the early church used to express that settled commitment to a specific local community of faith. Messaging the value of being in a lasting relationship with others that endures the highs and lows of the journey is part of planting like Jesus.

Reflect: What have you done to help people think clearly about membership or partnership with your ministry? What might you need to do to promote biblical clarity? What new steps might you need to take to help individuals commit to Jesus and to the kingdom vision of your ministry?

Prayer: *Christ, I thank you for your incarnate presence in and through your people by the Spirit. Draw us together as members of the body of Christ and partners in the gospel, I pray, for your great name's sake. Amen.*

✳ 35 ✳

HARD CONVERSATIONS

Read Matthew 14:31; 16:23; Galatians 2:11-21.

Immediately Jesus reached out his hand and caught him. "You of little faith," he said, "why did you doubt?"

—Matthew 14:31

I grew up in Minnesota, where we practice "Minnesota nice": Why have a blunt conversation when you can just pretend differences of opinion do not exist? The rule of thumb for teams may be to "form, storm, norm, and then perform,"[1] but Minnesotans and plenty of others are uncomfortable with the stormy phase. Some of us fear that talk too frank between people could destroy the ministry, while others of us fear that the organization can drift into dangerous denial without confronting the brutal facts. Consider the experience of Peter as a better alternative.

In the book of Galatians, there is a record of a moment when two leaders collided. Peter, front-row disciple of Jesus and prominent leader of the Jerusalem church, is confronted by Paul, an upstart innovative, intellectual pioneer who had his own encounter with Jesus on a Damascus road. Peter initially had been eating with uncircumcised Gentiles, thereby demonstrating the inclusive gospel of Jesus, which taught that Gentiles did not first need to adopt Jewish practices before they enter the kingdom of Christ. Peter accepted Jews and Gentiles equally in Christ. However, when certain Jewish friends of James, leader of the Jerusalem church, came along and looked upon Peter's practice with furrowed brows, Peter flipped. He dodged the criticism of these Jewish people by changing his view on Gentile conversion. He compromised a core gospel truth. It was that compromise that Paul locked onto and with which he confronted Peter. Paul opposed Peter eyeball to eyeball (see Galatians 2:11; note here that *Cephas* is Aramaic for *Peter*). This was not the first time Peter had been confronted about his behavior. Let's roll back the calendar a couple of years.

In the Gospels, Jesus has several confrontational encounters with Peter flowing out of his strong and affirming relationship with him. In Matthew 14:22-33, Peter is sinking after taking a few steps toward Jesus on the choppy water of Galilee. Jesus reaches out to rescue Peter while challenging him and his lack of faith. Much later, speaking to his face, Jesus has hard words for Peter in Matthew 16:23: "Get behind me, Satan! You are a stumbling block to me." Like Paul, Jesus does not shy away from confrontation when needed.

We can take a lesson from the style of Paul and of Jesus. They both spoke directly when the situation called for it. They did not talk about Peter among their associates. They did not triangulate or pit one side against the others, nor did they forever postpone a difficult talk. In each case, they spoke to Peter out of genuine affirming relationship and a desire to graciously correct. These were not "hit and run" conversations. In each case, Peter took the confrontation to heart and relationships grew stronger.

A planter friend named Gordon once talked with me about receiving a 360-degree evaluation. That experience involved the planter's selecting five close-working partners and asking them to frankly communicate their compliments and concerns regarding the planter's leadership through a confidential process. While not a face-to-face experience like the one Peter and Paul had, the exchange took place in the context of affirming relationship. It was a courageous choice by Gordon to invite others to help him look into his blind spots. To his credit, he received input without being defensive. He dropped his guard because he knew the intention was good.

Gordon illustrates a challenging conversation in the context of his receptivity. He was open to hearing hard words. Oftentimes, the conditions for our needing to share are not immediately welcoming. In those cases, we need to soften our approach (for example, "I have something

I need to ask you that may help us work better together. Would that be OK?"). We are often wise to use "I feel" statements rather than "You do" accusations and to own our part in the problem wherever we can. Ideally, you can frame the concern as a mutual challenge that calls for problem-solving rather than just assigning blame. In most every case, we are wise to ask questions along the way and to try to assume the best intentions rather than the worst. While Jesus may have had the insight to challenge Peter's motives, our abilities to do the same often fall short.

Planting is high-stakes work. Oftentimes, there are many investing in the effort and expectations are riding high. Under that pressure, the ability to communicate honestly and to receive input non-defensively is critical. Jesus and Peter show us this practice in real time.

Reflect: How are you doing with promoting honest and direct communication? What have you done recently to help you see into your blind spot? With whom do you need to speak graciously and directly this week?

Prayer: *Jesus, thank you for your great grace that is able to bring good from the toughest conversations. Help me not to fear engaging deeply with others when needed. Help me to speak and listen as you would have me do, I pray. Amen.*

✳ 36 ✳

IDENTIFYING LEADERS

Read John 2:13-22; Titus 1:5-9.

After [Jesus] was raised from the dead, his disciples recalled
what he had said. Then they believed the scripture and the
words that Jesus had spoken.

—John 2:22

Many people will naturally assume that spiritual leadership is what is practiced when someone takes on a role of some sort in a church. What could be more spiritual than being responsible for some activities at a church building or a religious organization? In start-up work, it is not uncommon to attract some people who have had a church experience in their past and who may be eager to have influence. This is an occupational hazard for planters. These folks may privately even aspire to some title or official role as indicating they are a leader. Such are the confusions and misperceptions that surround the issue of spiritual leadership. Look closely at the practice of Jesus and the early church, who had very different criteria when it came to spiritual leadership.

Jesus was always looking to matters of the heart as he formed his disciples for ministry, and it took time to cultivate the character qualities he wanted. It took considerable time to cultivate trust (see John 2:22), simple obedience (see John 6:1-13), reliability (see John 6:66-69), and servant attitude (see John 13:12-17). Jesus seems most attentive to his disciples' "why" and less concerned with the "how." He wants to develop their motives and attitudes. Those qualities of character would be essential to their future work. As Jesus' movement developed, the priority of personal character was recognized as the essential quality for future leaders, as evidenced in the Paul's letters to Timothy and Titus, where specific character traits are listed.

When Paul started a church-planting initiative on the island of Crete, he was taking on a particularly big challenge. In his brief letter to Titus, he writes how a prophet had warned that Cretans were notorious for being crude and rude: "'Cretans are always liars, vicious brutes, lazy gluttons'" (Titus 1:12). Wanting to establish a lasting witness to Jesus on Crete, Paul lifts up the theme of character in leadership. As Jesus had labored to instill qualities in the life of the Twelve, Paul encourages Titus to look for certain qualities in those whom he will ask to lead. Some of these qualities are clearly in contrast to what Paul indicates as the low morals of the local Cretans ("not quick-tempered, not given to drunkenness, not violent," v. 7). Others are very much in line with the character qualities Jesus instilled in his disciples ("hospitable, a lover of goodness, prudent, upright, devout, and self-controlled. He must have a firm grasp of the word . . ." vv. 8-9, NRSV). A similar list is found in 1 Timothy 3. The point is clear: While *doing* is an important step on the way to becoming a disciple, leadership is about *being*. Jesus and Paul point us to a qualitative step up. Leadership is a test of the unseen qualities of a person. Those quality essentials are usually developed over time, but they show up as invaluable to any start-up effort.

Sherry had her hands full with a young worship team whose members could not get along—too many people with too much talent and way too much ego. When the team gathered, the tension was thick. In the middle of this, she was given the responsibility to lead rehearsals. The temptations to be drawn into the petty offenses and strong personalities were weekly landmines. Sherry, however, was patient and not easily angered, two essential qualities in spiritual leadership. With some coaching help, she chose to establish a pattern of scripture meditation and prayer at the front end of the team's rehearsals and practice sessions. Sherry modeled the character of Jesus, which was both assertiveness and graciousness. In time, she gained the upper hand in setting a tone that turned around an unhealthy situation, and others in the worship band were captivated by her Christlike style and took a personal lesson from it. Everybody took a step up.

Church planters must exercise considerable caution when identifying leadership in their new ministries. Giving away tasks—not titles—is a way of testing character in real time as we get to know new people. Many a planter has made hasty or poor leadership choices, leading to regrets. We are looking for indications of character in keeping with the patterns of Jesus and the early church. Most of these people will need to be trained and mentored slowly, as Jesus did.

Patience in character formation as we develop spiritual leadership is integral to planting like Jesus.

Reflect: How are you keeping character central to leadership? Whom are you seeking to cultivate as a future leader? What is your plan to help them mature?

Prayer: *Lord of the church, as one under your authority, I want my leadership to reflect your lordship. Shape me into the character of Christ, and help me see and attend to those areas of my life that fall short, I pray. Amen.*

✳ 37 ✳

DEAD-END STREET OR
MULTIPLICATION HIGHWAY?

Read Luke 13:18-19; Acts 1:1-11.

> "What is the kingdom of God like? What shall I compare it
> to? It is like a mustard seed, which a man took and planted
> in his garden. It grew and became a tree, and the birds
> perched in its branches."
>
> —Luke 13:18-19

From the parable of the mustard seed, we have seen it is clear: Jesus intended for his kingdom to grow. Tracking the story of that expansion through the book of Acts reveals church planting mostly by accident. The followers of Jesus were scattered after Pentecost and then again after persecution (see Acts 8:1-4; 11:19), which led to the formation of new Jesus communities. In Acts 13, however, we have the first account of a church that moved from accidental planting to planned reproduction. When the Antioch church sent out Paul and Barnabas, they demonstrated the first intentional church planting effort. It was a breakthrough event.

Tracking the subsequent multiple church-planting mission trips of Paul takes us to Lystra, Derbe, Philippi, Thessalonica, Berea, Corinth, and Ephesus. In Ephesus, Paul puts down roots for two years. There, his teaching in the lecture hall of Tyrannus (see Acts 19:8-10) results in all the Jews and Greeks in Asia hearing the news of Jesus. Evidently, those two years of teaching (the first planting bootcamp?) released a wave of church planting across the region. Acts 19:10 is truly a remarkable commentary on the multiplication movement within the early Christian community. Reading the epistles through the eyes of the first recipients, we remember that they were instructional letters to new church leaders who were part of this remarkable movement. Paul travels and writes with a clear purpose: to establish new communities of Jesus followers who will witness to resurrection hope, truth, and power. He sees the kingdom as ever-expanding, from Jerusalem to Judea, to Samaria, and to the ends of the earth. Like cascading dominos in succession, Paul sees churches planting churches as the new normal.

From time to time, it is good to ask whether we have received the kingdom news as a dead-end street or as part of the multiplication highway. We may be wise to remember that after World War II, there was a great surge of church planting in the United States. Unfortunately, most of those churches did not see it as their mission to reproduce; and, as a result, the planting movement slowed dramatically throughout the 1960s, 1970s, and 1980s. As a consequence of this, the collective church-planting memory within churches and denominations was nearly lost. Few people had any experience in planting, and so the great majority were like "a deer in the headlights" when the thought of starting a new Christian community was suggested. Thankfully, the spark to multiply is being rekindled today in many places. You are likely part of that new flame.

Jeff was pastoring a suburban congregation in Kalamazoo, Michigan, when he felt the challenge to multiply. Partnering with a local campus minister, the congregation planted in a part of the city that otherwise Jeff never would have been able to reach. One day, to his delight, he discovered that the new church that was reaching into the college community of his city was feeling a prompt to launch an urban congregation. This too would extend a witness into a part of the city that was underserved by any church. So, Jeff and his colleagues teamed up with an urban street ministry, and, by God's grace, that urban ministry launched successfully. Jeff's original vision for one new church had become two. Imagine the joy he and his congregation felt when that urban street minister carried the vision forward to start ministries in Benton Harbor, Michigan, and then in Detroit. Jeff's story is an example of how Christ comes to us on the way to someone else. These congregations would not settle for being a dead-end street, and that vision was contagious.

We get to choose whether the kingdom movement stops with us or not. Some have observed that new churches that multiply before they ever own property of their own tend to grow faster and larger. Stories like that of Jeff illustrate the point: We get to write our own narrative as the Spirit leads us into the mustard seed-kingdom. Orienting ourselves toward the multiplication highway is planting like Jesus.

Reflect: What is God saying to you as you reflect upon your ministry and the greater vision of Jesus in Acts 1:8? What might you do to intentionality take steps to be a multiplying church? Who else might you need to include to join you as keeper of the vision to multiply?

Prayer: *Risen Christ, I hear your call to make disciples of all peoples. Thank you for those who invested in my life for that cause. Help me to lead in such a way that my ministry is a highway for new disciples, new leaders, and new churches reaching new places, I pray. Amen.*

❈ 38 ❈

DEVELOPING GENEROUS GIVERS

Read Matthew 6:19-21; 1 Timothy 6:17-19.

"Where your treasure is, there your heart will be also."

—Matthew 6:21

Left to ourselves, we all tend to accumulate stuff. We collect clothes, cars, tools, toys, gadgets, and, above all, we tend to collect money. In all of that accumulation, we tend to use the possessive pronoun liberally: *my* house, *my* couch, *my* trailer, *my* money. All of this possessive talk that falls so easily from our lips, however, runs contrary to the basic biblical teaching that God is the ultimate owner of all things. Psalm 24 teaches that "the earth is the LORD's" (v. 1 and following), anchoring that claim in God's creative acts: because God "founded it on the seas and established it upon the waters" (v. 2). That makes claiming ownership in our casual use of pronouns a bit outrageous. God actually owning it all is a big-time game changer in our possession-minded culture today. Ponder that!

In 1 Timothy, Paul is instructing his protégé Timothy as he develops the recently planted church in Ephesus. In that instruction, he speaks frankly about the development of generosity. First, he uses an imperative when he tells Timothy to "command them" (1 Tim. 6:17-18). Paul is not expecting Timothy to demand or force so much as he wants Timothy to be *intentional*. He knows that people do not and will not shift their perspective easily. Paul has already given Timothy considerable teaching material on the riskiness of building a life upon the acquisition of wealth (see 1 Timothy 6:6-10). In this, he reflects the teaching of Jesus, who warned against the power of material goods to enslave the human heart (see Matthew 6:21). Notice, Jesus does not say our heart predicts where our treasure will go, though that may be true. He actually says the opposite—that where our treasures go tends to predict a heart outcome. Paul names that unfortunate outcome, where love of money is a priority, as being "a trap" (1 Tim. 6:9).

Second, Paul again uses the imperative with Timothy, urging him to be deliberate about teaching people to give (see 1 Timothy 6:18). Generosity does not come naturally or intuitively; it must be taught. Left to ourselves, we revert to our possessive pronoun, *mine*, like a two-year-old with a favorite toy. Timothy is to challenge people to be generous and willing to share, with an eye for the significant blessing that act can be, "thus storing up for themselves the treasure of a good foundation for the future, so that they may take hold of the life that really is life" (1 Tim. 6:19, NRSV). There is an abundant life to be entered into through the practice of generosity. As Jesus said, "It is more blessed to give than to receive" (Acts 20:35).

Sean is a friend and planter who came to me on one occasion with a tough story. His church plant was growing but was in serious financial trouble. He needed more help from the denomination and assumed that given the good growth they were experiencing, he likely would qualify for a generous funding grant. I recall that conversation, as I challenged him first to go to his congregation with full transparency regarding the need. I reminded Sean that people revert to "mine" and that you must teach them to see everything as belonging ultimately to God and then also teach them to be generous in the ministry they share. Sean did just that. He taught biblical stewardship, and he began to share unapologetically their vision for community impact, along with the cost of that effort, and then to report every month the congregation's progress in giving. In addition, the congregation changed their practice from placing a passive collection box by the door to having a weekly collection, in which Sean set an example by stepping forward as the offering basket was passed to put his check into the collection. A few short months later, Sean called me back, saying that God had met their congregation's need; they would not need more denominational funds. Lesson learned.

Generosity must be taught. By nature, we tend toward possessiveness. Those possessive pronouns creep into our vocabulary quickly. It is our responsibility as developers of a new ministry to take the lead by example and by instruction and thereby to grow generous givers. Paul gave this strong instruction to a church planter, and we must receive it too if we will plant like Jesus.

Reflect: What might be holding you back in fully accepting the responsibility to grow generous givers in your ministry? How is God growing you in generosity? What steps toward generous giving might you need to take with your community?

Prayer: *Lord Jesus, we are mindful of your generosity, as you were rich yet became poor for our sake. Teach me to take hold of abundant life through greater generosity, and use me to prompt others to grow in the grace of giving. Amen.*

⁜ 39 ⁜

BALANCING YOUR TEAM

Read Acts 1:1-8; Ephesians 4:11-16.

"You will receive power when the Holy Spirit comes on you;
and you will be my witnesses in Jerusalem, and in all Judea
and Samaria, and to the ends of the earth."

—Acts 1:8

So much of church planting is about balance. The planting life can consume every waking hour, but our personal lives will be with us when we are old and gray. Best not to neglect our families. Best to be balanced. Our ministries require time for meetings, personal study and prayer, leader training, and pastoral visits, while our communities present opportunities for service, networking, and witness. Best not neglect any of these areas; best to be balanced. Balancing time and energy is a daily challenge. In his book 5Q: *Reactivating the Original Intelligence and Capacity of the Body of Christ*, Alan Hirsch reminds us that Ephesians 4 presents another critical balancing act with the five essential equipping gifts.[1]

The five gifts from the risen Christ, according to Ephesians, are "the apostles, the prophets, the evangelists, the pastors and teachers" (4:11). If we reflect upon these gifts, we will see the very character of our Lord. Was Jesus a great teacher? Yes, he was. Jesus taught with authority and had a great grasp of the scriptures. Was Jesus a great pastor/shepherd? Yes, he was. He took up the sick and the outcast into his care and attention. Was Jesus a great evangelist? Yes, he was. Jesus announced the kingdom and invited people into his reign at most every turn; he was always inviting people to follow him. Was Jesus a great prophet? Yes, he was. Jesus spoke truth to power with the religious and political leaders of his day. What Jesus a great apostle? Yes, he was. Jesus was sent by God into the world and lived that mission faithfully unto death on a cross. When we look at the gifts the risen Christ has given us, we see quickly that they make up the very character of Jesus. Jesus has given us his Spirit in such a way that the body of Christ has the fullness of the gifts of Jesus. Jesus told of this at his ascension, when he predicted in Acts 1:8 the coming of the Spirit with power for kingdom mission.

What does this mean for church planters who are balancing work, family, ministry, and mission? It means that if we are self-aware, we will develop a team to counter our strengths and weaknesses. It means that we should be on the lookout for the gifted people God brings to us, to see how we can build a team that reflects the fivefold gifts of Ephesians 4:11. It means that some people who may be sitting on the sidelines should, on our invitation, get into the game because they have equipping gifts that are not represented in our ministry.

What if it is true that the words of Ephesians 4:11 represent the "genetic code" of the body of Christ? What if it is true that the five-fold gifting for apostles, prophets, evangelists, pastors, and teachers is the earliest blueprint for ministry design, found first in Jesus and outlined retrospectively by Paul? Imagine the potential insight that is here for designing our work, setting our ministry priorities, and organizing our structure! We begin with an understanding of the design that comes from the head of the church, Jesus (see Ephesians 4:15-16), coupled with an honest assessment of the gifts represented on our team. From here, we can begin to see the path whereby we reflect "the full stature of Christ" (v. 13). All of this becomes very practical in real time.

Mike is a guy with amazing apostolic and evangelistic gifts. Those gifts needed to be highlighted in planting, which is good. When churches turn inward and fail to grow, it is often because apostolic and evangelistic gifts are ignored. However, a team that is led by an apostolic evangelist like Mike needs a person with shepherding gifts on that team (or personal needs and concerns can be overlooked, resulting in people getting hurt), just like a team led by a shepherd needs a person with apostolic gifts on that team (or people tend to turn inward and lose sight of the mission). Mike also needed a prophetic person on the team to represent the important justice and mercy issues in the community (without whom, again, the team can lose sight of its social witness). The fivefold gifts gave an overall healthy balance to the priorities of the team. The fullness potential of our Lord Jesus was present, and blind spots where the presence of Jesus is needed were reduced.

Finally, the purpose of these gifts of the Spirit is to equip. A team of five-fold Ephesians 4:11 representative leaders should see themselves as responsible for training others into those areas, and not do it all themselves. This must be part of what Jesus meant when he identified the coming of the Spirit with power. The equipping gifts of the Spirit activate the body of Christ for kingdom work. This is the way our church can come to "the whole measure of the fullness of Christ" (v. 13). A balanced team of equippers who plant in the spirit of Jesus is a prescription for less stress as responsibility is distributed, greater efficiency as people work in their gift areas, and fewer failures as blind spots are reduced. This is good news for those who desire to plant like Jesus.

Reflect: How aware are you of your weak areas in spiritual gifting? How have you done in creating space for all the equipping gifts of the Spirit? What further steps do you need to take?

Prayer: *Spirit of the risen Christ, I thank you for the equipping gifts you have given. Help me see and make room for those who are gifted to empower others to serve. Bring to fullness the presence of Christ through the gifts you have given, I pray. Amen.*

❊ 40 ❊

SYSTEM TUNE-UP

Read Luke 5:36-39; Acts 6:1-7.

> *"No one tears a piece out of a new garment to patch an old one. Otherwise, they will have torn the new garment, and the patch from the new will not match the old."*
>
> —Luke 5:36

Leader development and organizational development are linked together. When leaders grow more effective, their number of followers tends to increase, and the system designed in the beginning is no longer adequate. The organizational friction that results can be referred to as "growing pains": Decision-making has become too clumsy; communications are now inadequate; alignment is "fuzzy." When we begin to feel that "this-is-not-working-anymore" type of feeling, it may be time to step back from working *in* the church and begin to work *on* the church. Jesus alludes to the need for systemic change in the parable of the garment in Luke 5. An old design solution to a new dynamic development is all too often backwards thinking. The book of Acts outlines a particular tune-up episode in our reading today that illustrates the point.

Acts 6 begins with a significant statement: "The number of disciples was increasing" (v. 1). That good growth, however, was creating a problem for the Twelve, as they had been taking responsibility for all of the teaching as well as providing for the needs of the widows. As the pressure for their time and attention grew, church leadership evidently failed to deliver food to some Greek-speaking Jewish widows. Not a good thing! What followed was some restructuring of the organization, so that the Twelve could give their time fully to their teaching work and others would take responsibility for distributing food to deserving widows. It was a classic division-of-labor strategy that released pressure from a few and distributed responsibility more widely within the organization. With the help of the deacons who took on service projects (see Acts 6:2—*diakonia* translates as "to wait upon"), the Twelve were able focus on teaching, and the result was rapid growth (see Acts 6:7).

This story has a parallel in Exodus 18, where Moses is confronted by his father-in-law, Jethro. In this incident, Moses is taking all the responsibility for helping to settle disputes between people. The text says he is working at that task every day, from morning until evening; sounds exhausting! Little wonder that Jethro speaks to Moses these direct words: "What you are doing is not good" (Exod. 18:17). Jethro got right to the point, and for good reason: He saw that Moses was in trouble and about to burn out. There had to be a better way.

After several years up to his elbows in planting work, Tyler came to realize that he was tired and feeling rather exhausted. Through a time of reflection, he was challenged to draft an organizational chart that outlined all the key leaders and their lines of accountability. That exercise helped him see that he had twenty-three people reporting to him; no wonder he was feeling drained! His team agreed that system was not working and needed to change. After reorganizing the lines of accountability so that he had only half as many reporting relationships, he began to feel considerable relief, and more got done. The restructuring did require time in training people and establishing new systems. Tyler had to release authority in some areas where he could delegate, but the payoff was well worth it.

Church plants require regular system tune-ups. Organizations must adapt to new circumstances, new growth, and new challenges. Like Tyler, none of us does well over the long haul when we carry more responsibilities than we should. As multipliers, we do better to offload duties through raising up new disciples and leaders. It is a practice as old as Moses and the early church. Even Jesus acknowledged this need for organizational and structural change, when he talked about the need for new wineskins in which to pour new wine (see Luke 5:37-39). Just as the good news of the kingdom could not be forced into older religious systems, the good progress we make in ministry cannot forever be forced into the same systems. The systems of a ministry must always be in service to the purpose of the organization, never the other way around. This too is part of planting like Jesus.

Reflect: Where in your ministry do you feel that your system is no longer adequate for your mission? How are you feeling that poor fit? What might you need to do, and what are the next important steps?

Prayer: *Lord, save me from trying to do too much, and help me grow others as leaders. Help me discern how my style and our ministry systems may need to change to reach our full potential. This is your church, Jesus; I release it to you. Amen.*

Part 3

Daily Readings on
Leadership Effectiveness Like Jesus

❧ 41 ❧

BE FILLED WITH THE SPIRIT

Read Mark 1:7-8; Ephesians 5:15-20.

"After me comes the one more powerful than I, the straps of whose sandals I am not worthy to stoop down and untie. I baptize you with water, but he will baptize you with the Holy Spirit."

—Mark 1:7-8

Jesus and the early followers said a lot about the work of the Spirit in the mission of God. Jesus began his ministry with the anointing of the Spirit (see Luke 3:21-22) and made it known through John that he would baptize us with the Holy Spirit (see Mark 1:8). He did ministry in the power of the Spirit (see Luke 4:14 and following), and he preached and healed in the power of the Spirit (see Matthew 12:18, 28). Our Lord predicted the coming of the Spirit as our indwelling helper (see John 14:16-20) and guide into the truth (see John 16:12-14). This is the same Spirit that Jesus indicated would connect us profoundly to himself by baptism and would come upon us with power for witness to the ends of the earth (see Acts 1:5-8). Clearly, we cannot expect to plant like Jesus if we fail to seek and know the presence and power of the Holy Spirit.

While not all followers of Jesus express how they experience the power and presence of the Holy Spirit in the same way, most would agree that there is a dimension to this reality that is conditional or episodic. We may know the settled reality of the baptism of the Spirit in which we are wholly and mysteriously fused to Christ, while we may also know the times in our ministry when we were filled uniquely and powerfully with the Spirit for some specific purpose. We may also be keenly aware of those times when we were not Spirit-filled. For example, there is a frequent connection between verbal witness to the gospel and the filling of the Spirit (see Acts 2:4; 4:31; Ephesians 5:18-19). Some of us may witness to that experience when we proclaim Christ publicly. Jesus references that filling of the Spirit for witness in Mark 13:11 in the circumstances of persecution. That same filling is an empowering that Jesus himself experienced in the wilderness and that strengthened him against temptation (see Luke 4:1-13). It is an empowering that we can seek and experience. The letters of Paul warn us several times against suppressing (see 1 Thessalonians 5:4-10) or offending that work of the Spirit. The filling of the Spirit is a precious empowering for ministry not to be minimized.

Some time ago, a theological seminary professor broke all the rules (a nice thought!) and did a practicum on the power and filling of the Spirit. It was an experiential learning experiment that had a profound impact upon many students who had never prayed seeking the filling of the Spirit nor seen the manifestations of the power of the Holy Spirit. Healings and prophecies were present. Words of wisdom and prophecy were spoken. It was powerful, and it upset some theological assumptions. In time, apprehension shifted to receptivity, and then to yearning: Holy Spirit, come! Those students received a powerful resource for their future ministry when they faced the inevitable challenges and adversities that come.

By now, most of us know that church planting is terribly difficult work. Just the time we think we have things in hand, we don't. We are up against challenges that, despite our greatest efforts, feel impossible. An obstinate person who seems intent on sabotaging our work; a sudden illness, when we have been healthy for years; a sense that no one is receptive to our presence; personal and private struggles with depression; or a profound moral setback in our already fragile team; we cannot do this without the filling of the Spirit. We cannot do this without regular prayers: "Lord, fill me with your Spirit, the very Spirit of Jesus today . . . this moment . . . this hour . . . in this meeting . . . in this work!"

In the year 1054 AD, church leaders were engaged by a significant question known as the Filioque controversy. The concern was to determine whether the Holy Spirit proceeds from God alone (one person of the Trinity) or whether the Spirit proceeds from both God and Christ (two persons of the Trinity). (This hardly sounds controversial by our standards today!) The western church settled on texts that seemed to indicate both (see Matthew 10:20; John 16:7; Galatians 4:6). The Spirit we seek is the Spirit of God and of Jesus. Jesus said he would send that very Spirit to us. We can do our work in the power and with the filling of the Spirit of Jesus, who showed us how to demonstrate and declare the kingdom of God.

The work of the Spirit is indispensable to the mission of God and is therefore essential to planting like Jesus. Perhaps this powerful dynamic has been "layered over" with task lists and project plans. If so, today is the day to seek the filling of the Spirit.

Reflect: In the quietness of wherever you are, open your heart to the Spirit, seeking a fresh filling. What do you hear that may need to be confessed, received, or obeyed? How might this prayer become a regular practice? When might you need to teach your planting team about the filling of the Spirit? How would you go about that?

Prayer: *Spirit of the Living God, fill me for your work. Fill me to witness to the reality of the resurrected Lord Jesus. Fill me to follow you deeper into your mission. Fill me to hear your voice and obey completely. Amen.*

✳ 42 ✳

PREVENIENT GRACE

Read John 1:1-9; 12:32.

> *The true light that gives light to everyone was coming into the world.*
>
> —John 1:9

There is hardly a more-encouraging truth to anyone who would greatly risk to start a new Christian community reaching new people than the truth of prevenient grace. Some days, we wake up to a wall: It seems as if nothing is happening and that all our efforts for weeks have been fruitless. We can easily just roll over in bed or slump down in our chair, defeated. But look again at what scripture teaches us about God's advancing grace and what this can mean for church planting. This is truly some of the best "good news" spiritual pioneers rely upon!

In the Old Testament, God calls Adam in the garden while he is hiding from God. God also calls Abraham out of his father's house in Haran, Moses while he is tending a flock, and Jacob for no good reason of his own. Later, the unmistakable call of God comes to Deborah and Esther in a time of national need; Mary, as a humble woman and mother of Jesus; and Lydia, as a local business leader who becomes the first to embrace a new church vision for Philippi. Sit with any of these individuals. These major figures from the Hebrew and Christian scriptures establish the initiating work of God as a pattern. It is a theme that only continues and deepens into the New Testament. God is the initiator in spiritual awakenings, not us. We love God only because God first loved us and pursues

God's creation with grace (see 1 John 4:19). Jesus embodies the God who is a loving initiator seeking to save the lost (see Luke 19:10).

The profound reality of God's initiating work is communicated in several key texts. The Gospel of John identifies this reality with words such as these: "The true light that gives light to everyone was coming into the world" (John 1:9); and "I, when I am lifted up from the earth, will draw all people to myself" (John 12:32). Paul speaks of this broad, pursuing grace in Acts 17:26-27, when he makes his appeal in Athens; and again, in Titus 2:11-14, citing "all people" as receiving the grace of God (v. 11). It is particularly worth noting that Paul extends that prevenient work of grace to the challenging mission field of Crete, where Titus is ministering. In these texts, we see how the presence of God in all places and all times is preparing the world for hearing and responding to the good news of Jesus. John Wesley called it "prevenient grace" or "prior grace."

Many of us have had conversations with people who are in some way annoyed with church, yet curious about or even admiring of Jesus. Kent is a millennial friend who is very much in that frame of mind. Most every exposure he has had with church has left him cold; meanwhile, Jesus stirs his admiration. He is drawn to the Jesus who stands for the poor and the outsider. Recently, he even told me that he has a fondness for some Christian hymns. Kent will likely not walk through the door of an established church anytime soon, but he clearly has the tug of prevenient grace at work within him. At some point, I predict he will cross a line; perhaps it will be through a trusted friend who invites him or at some point in a new season of his life. I am waiting with confidence. I just know that God is at work in his life, long before I get involved.

Discovering the kernel of grace that is germinating within a human soul often requires that we set aside the "church conversation." The shortest distance from where a person is at spiritually to where we might like them to be is rarely a straight line. But there are other conversations we can have that feed the hunger of the soul. Jesus modeled these in his work with people in his ministry. We may find our work more fruitful if we follow that example too. Talking about spiritual values and practices may be more meaningful, as Paul did in Athens (see Acts 17:22). Another tack is to go straight to the experiential domain, asking, "May I share with you my experience with Jesus?" You might even follow up with the question, "What has been your experience with Jesus?" Jesus always first, and church sometime later.

However slow progress may feel at times, we take fresh encouragement from the reality that God is the One who is initiating. We are not the primary carriers of the good news; God is the One who is whispering the hope of a purposeful and abundant life into the hearts of people. God is the One who creates a heartfelt hunger for forgiveness, justice, reconciliation, and healing. God has set God's affections upon our neighbors and communities long before we showed up. Acknowledging that work is how we plant like Jesus.

Reflect: How does the reality of prevenient grace challenge you to rethink the toughest areas of your work? What indicators of prevenient grace do you see at work around you, and how can you best partner with God in those places? How does this biblical principle alter your approach to planting?

Prayer: *Lord of all peoples, I thank you for your vast love and desire to seek and redeem. Show me how you are drawing people to yourself in my neighborhood and community, that I might participate with you fully in that work, for Jesus' sake. Amen.*

❖ 43 ❖

DEMYTHOLOGIZING

Read John 4:27-37.

> *"Don't you have a saying, 'It's still four months until har-*
> *vest'? I tell you, open your eyes and look at the fields! They*
> *are ripe for harvest."*
>
> —John 4:35

Have you ever felt you were "thrown off your game"? Sometimes it is physical burnout and we are exhausted, needing rest; time for a vacation. Other times, it is a mental thing that worms its way into our head, and we wonder why we feel exhausted or lose heart. Such mental harassment can mess with us in click-bait we might read, such as, "The church in America will disappear in a generation" or "The United States is becoming a nation of atheists and agnostics." Not exactly the kind of mental food that motivates us to get out of bed. These are the half-truths and speculations (not entirely uncommon, I would add) that have the potential to suck up all the mental oxygen, leaving us gasping for kingdom truth and hope.

Jesus and the New Testament writers often had to correct misunderstandings that had burrowed into the early followers' thinking, so we can hear them counter with words such as "do not think . . ." or "think not . . ." (Matthew 5:17; Romans 12:3; 1 Peter 4:12). In John 4, Jesus issues a mental correction for his disciples. They had been thinking of their kingdom harvest work as they would think of any other farming venture. They expected a season of planting and then a season of waiting until the harvest was ready. They assumed that the waiting for harvest was going to take considerable time, as agricultural cycles tend to require. Jesus, by contrast, speaks to them fresh off an encounter with a woman who had immediately responded to him and, in turn, invited her friends to meet him. He wants his disciples to feel a sense of urgency and optimism. They are thinking that the harvest is far off; but Jesus sees harvest as an immediate opportunity, when he says to them, "Don't you have a saying, 'It's still four months until harvest'? I tell you, open your eyes and look at the fields! They are ripe for harvest" (John 4:35). Jesus is challenging their assumptions as relates to future kingdom work. They imagine there will be four months to lie around and do little else; Jesus wants them to see that their circumstances are actually ideal for results now. They had drawn their assumptions and conclusions before really looking at things and seeing the ready-to-pick potential in the fields.

So often, a slight error in our thinking can have a profound impact upon our work, even to the point of defeating us. These are the lies and half-truths that find their ways into our heads and drain away our energy and motivation. I live in West Michigan, home of several Christian colleges, a variety of faith-based publishing houses, and churches on what seems to be every city block. This part of the country is blessed with religious broadcasting and a great many faith-based nonprofits. In recent years, several start-up congregations have ballooned into megachurch size, with thousands attending. As a result, many dismiss the idea of further planting in my town because it is presumed to be over-churched and not a good risk for start-up ventures.

My friend Larry, however, came with a fresh set of eyes. He saw the predicament of those who struggled with recovery from addiction: They could not find a church that understood their profound predicament and spoke their language. Evergreen Ministries stepped into that gap, and the harvest has been remarkably plentiful. Larry, through his experiences, illustrates the teaching of Jesus: The harvest is plentiful, if only we can see it.

Why do we let negative myths settle into our minds? There are probably many reasons. Planting is hard work, and when things do not progress positively, it is tempting to reach for an explanation or excuse. It could be that we have tuned into a negative messenger and, over time, that negative message has bored itself into our minds like a nasty computer virus. It could be that negative narrative has crowded out the kingdom narrative we once carried foremost in our minds.

Today, Jesus comes with a fresh word of hope and challenge. He calls us out of a defeatist mental loop, busting up some myths, as he did with the disciples: "You have a saying . . . [but] I tell you, open your eyes!" That is the good news empowering us to plant like Jesus.

Reflect: What are the thoughts that most often circulate in your mind that drain away your energy and become a source of discouragement? What would Jesus say about those thoughts? Where do you see hopeful signs of future harvest? What might you do to keep a kingdom narrative foremost in your mind?

Prayer: *Lord of this day and this ministry, teach me to trust you, one step at a time, with what I am called to do. Guard my heart and mind against negative thoughts. Lead me by your Spirit of hope, in Jesus' name. Amen.*

⊱ 44 ⊰

AN ABUNDANCE MENTALITY

Read Matthew 6:25-34; Genesis 2:4-15.

*"But seek first his kingdom and his righteousness, and all
these things will be given to you as well."*

—Matthew 6:33

One of the most basic questions to settle in ministry is the question
of abundance: Put simply, are there enough resources to provide for
our need? A scarcity mentality would cause us to be overly concerned, to
the point of curtailing our plans, surrendering our vision, and closing up
shop—not enough money to pay the utilities or the rent or the staff. With
a scarcity mindset comes chronic anxiety and worry about things, to the
extent that we take our eyes off of productive work to grow the kingdom.
Worry can paralyze us at just the time when action is needed.

Is there an antidote to scarcity thinking? Genesis provides an answer
to scarcity anxiety. The Bible begins by asserting God as Creator and
therefore God as owner of all things. Psalm 24 says it this way: "The earth
is the LORD's and all that is in it, the world, and those who live in it; for
he has founded it on the seas, and established it on the rivers" (Ps. 24:1-2,
NRSV). God owns it all. God owns all the resources, all the provisions, all
the funding, all the dollars. As Creator, God owns it all; therefore, there
is no shortage of resources. So what is the problem here?

Genesis goes on to give us a significant clue. The writer of Genesis places humankind in the garden, bearing the image of God. In the
ancient world, readers would have understood that in a certain way. They

knew how emperors over a vast domain would erect images of themselves at the farthest reaches of the empire to signal to all others the rightful ownership of the land. That image was a signal to others: Whatever grand illusions they may have as to their ownership, the rightful owner is represented by the sovereign's visible image. When Genesis teaches that we have been made in the image of God, the teaching is that we are not the owners. No, instead, we signal the reality of a rightful sovereign. We are temporary managers, while God owns it all. The biblical word for our temporary status as caretaker is *steward*.

Tyler was more than two years into planting a new faith community in an urban area of Minneapolis that had become a magnet for millennials. Part of the identity he has woven into his ministry is that of environmental stewardship. When we met to talk about his budget, he reported that he had three regular givers, in addition to himself. We agreed that this needed to change. So Tyler began to talk with his people about ownership and about stewardship as it relates to personal generosity. In a few short months, he had more than twenty regular givers. While their total weekly offerings were still modest (most givers start that way), we agreed that he had hit upon a truth—the principle of stewardship—that people were able to hear and receive. Let's look at the Creation story once more.

In Genesis, the image bearers are commissioned to care for the creation. The phrase "to work it and take care of it" (Gen. 2:15) carries with it the idea of stewarding temporarily that which does not actually belong to us. God remains the rightful owner, while the management or stewardship of the creation has been given over to humanity. While there is no shortage of resources for the mission of God, there may be a shortage of stewardship-minded people.

That stingy ownership mentality, however, can be changed, as Tyler illustrated. There may be a shortage of generous givers today who recognize their rightful role not as owners but as temporary managers of creation. Generosity, however, can be developed. *Stewardship* was a word that Tyler's millennial friends heard with open ears. It is a practice with broad application, including stewardship of the environment, time, resources, and finances.

Anxiety about money is not a good thing. Jesus counsels us in Matthew 6, "Therefore I tell you, do not worry . . . but strive first for the kingdom" (Matthew 6:25, 33). Better to put our attention on developing kingdom values and practices; better to help people shift from ownership to stewardship. Stewardship development is integral to planting like Jesus.

Reflect: Do you come at your ministry with mostly a scarcity mentality or an abundance mentality; and why do you think this is so? How would you function differently if you consistently had an abundance/stewardship frame of mind? How can you cultivate generosity in your community?

Prayer: *Lord of all creation, your resources are vast and beyond my imagination. Empower me to make disciples who understand their place as stewards of what is only temporarily theirs. Give me peace in your amazing provision, I pray. Amen.*

✤ 45 ✤

ENJOY THE RIDE!

Read Matthew 13:44; 2 Corinthians 8:1-4.

> *"The kingdom of heaven is like treasure hidden in a field.*
> *When a man found it, he hid it again, and then in his joy*
> *went and sold all he had and bought that field."*
>
> —Matthew 13:44

Church-planting leadership was never meant to be sustained by sheer willpower. This work cannot be done long term through grinding self-discipline and long hours. There must be a source of energy, drive, and renewal that comes from a deeper place and that keeps us returning to the challenges. There should be something more others see than a hardworking visionary leader. There should be a profound motivation and reserve. That palpable energy should lift our hearts on days even when the climb is steep. It should quiet our minds after a long day when our head finally hits the pillow.

Jesus takes us to that deeper place in John 15: "I have told you this so that my joy may be in you and that your joy may be complete" (v. 11). Jesus never expected us to do kingdom work without the joy he provides. In the verses surrounding verse 11, Jesus directs us to the practices of love. Following Jesus in his ethic of unconditional love as both a receiver and a giver is a central way we can enter into his joy. "Joy," as Chesterton has written, "is the gigantic secret of the Christian," and that joy is indispensable in church planting.[1]

Jason is a parachute planter in North Dakota. He began his work with humble community-engagement strategies such as providing blankets for people who were homeless and shoveling out fire hydrants that were covered in February snowdrifts. You could see and feel the joy Jason had on his face and in his soul as he circled up another team of people for each service project he hatched from his home. Love is a shortcut to joy, and I watched him as he fed upon that energy through the early, tough stages of church planting; it kept his heart light, even when projects would stumble. And some did stumble. The word, however, began to spread about his service projects, and the joyous enthusiasm was magnetic. Multiply those service projects over the course of several months, and when summer finally arrived and the ice thawed, he celebrated more than twenty baptisms, long before he began public worship. Imagine the simile on Jason's face!

Church planter and apostle Paul often directed his young churches to this source of inner renewal. In 2 Corinthians 1:24, he shares with the church he labored to plant the encouragement that "we work with you for your joy." Later in 2 Corinthians, he describes the joy of another community of disciples in their sacrificial service to a suffering church needing help, with "their overflowing joy and their extreme poverty welled up in rich generosity" (8:2). What he describes there is not so much a great sacrifice but a great joy *in* sacrifice. Paul called out this quality of joy, and he wanted his churches to know deep delight in God and in kingdom participation.

The Bible is full of references to being joyful. Texts tie joy to worship: "Rejoice in the Lord" (Phil. 4:4); to scripture: "The precepts of the LORD are right, rejoicing the heart" (Ps. 19:8, NRSV); to prayer: "Ask and you will receive, so that your joy may be complete" (John 16:24, NRSV); and to generosity: "'It is more blessed to give than to receive'" (Acts 20:35). Jesus ultimately points to his kingdom as a treasure of joy: "The kingdom of heaven is like treasure hidden in a field. When a man found it, he hid it again, and then in his joy went and sold all he had and bought that field" (Matt. 13:44). It has been stated often that joy is the unmistakable mark of the Christian. For this reason alone, it must be a distinguishing mark of planting work. We may not have a building or a worship band or much of a bank account, but if we have joy in our work, we have what the world cannot give. As a kingdom pioneer, know the permission of heaven to express that joy!

Jesus is not asking that we pump up ourselves or others into a giddy, emotional bubble; our Lord himself demonstrated the whole range of human emotions, normally and naturally. But under the pressure and in the quiet places, he carried with him a joy that he wants to give us. C. S. Lewis said, "There is a kind of happiness and wonder that makes you serious."[2] It is a joy in Jesus himself and in his kingdom and in his abiding presence. It is a joy that God is for us and is working for our good. It is a joy that will lift our hearts when the road is tough, and it is a joy that will draw others toward Jesus.

Enjoy the ride!

Reflect: How is it with your soul today? How can you find your way to the peace and joy of Christ in the midst of your work? What promise from God can you claim to recover kingdom joy?

Prayer: *Lord Jesus, I thank you that you are always at work for my good, always the lover of my life and soul, always with me and working through me. Fill me with your spirit of joy. I delight in who you are as a holy, good, and gracious Savior. Amen.*

❖ 46 ❖

SAFE IS NOT SAFE

Read Matthew 25:14-30.

> *"Whoever has will be given more, and they will have an abundance. Whoever does not have, even what they have will be taken from them."*
>
> —Matthew 25:29

Have you ever awoken to a new day with an overwhelming urge to put everything you have worked for into reverse? I am talking about the day after that day when nothing went right. One of your key leaders just quit, your landlord announced an increase in your rent, the financial team recommended budget cuts, and there is conflict within your worship team. Ugh! Under circumstances half this crazy, who could blame you for wanting to retreat to a safer spot in ministry? What could be so bad about finding a sleepy little kingdom assignment somewhere very far from here? Jesus has counsel for that very understandable wish.

In Matthew 25, our Lord tells a story of three servants who receive sizable investments from their master, who is leaving town. Each is entrusted with a different amount, according to their ability. Upon his return, the master comes to collect his investment and finds that two of the three have turned a profit on their portion, and they are rewarded for their due diligence. The third servant, however, indicates that he has made a very different choice than the others, based upon a perception of the master: "Master, I knew that you were a harsh man, reaping where you did not sow, and gathering where you did not scatter seed; so I was afraid, and I went and hid your talent in the ground" (Matt. 25:24-25, NRSV). This does not sit well with the master, who reprimands the servant, saying that he expected a return on his investment and that punishment for the servant's failure to provide one will be severe.

If you pause to think about it, the actions of the third servant make no sense whatsoever: If he did know that the master expected a return on his investment, why would he bury the gold in the ground where it would yield nothing? The only explanation that makes any sense is that the servant did not grasp the master's expectation that he must risk something in order to see a potential gain. That place where he had buried the bag of gold, which felt safe to the third servant, was actually not safe at all. Hiding the gold in the ground entailed no risk and therefore held no potential for reward. Jesus is teaching his followers here that being part of his movement requires a measure of risk for the sake of desired kingdom gains. The Master desires to "gather where he did not sow" (v. 24, adapted). It's an expectation that snaps our escapist daydreaming back to kingdom reality.

Perhaps you have heard the saying "Don't doubt in the dark what God has shown you in the light." We all have times when things look gloomy. In those times, we may wish for a safer place. This story, however, reminds us God intends that we take the gifts we have been given and risk them in kingdom ventures. That wish to retreat to an easier or safer place that we have from time to time can be a very normal indicator that we are exactly where God wants us to be. John the Baptist has a similar bout with doubts when, after his rather risky work (preaching repentance to King Herod) has gotten him thrown into prison, he wonders about the identity of Jesus. His doubts come long after he has baptized Jesus and seen his power: "Are you the one who is to come, or should we expect someone else?" (Matt. 11:3). John has put a great deal on the line in his prophetic calling; and now, from prison, he is overcome with a wave of uncertainty.

If John knew some anxiety, it is understandable that there may be occasions when we have similar bouts of doubt. Any new initiative, particularly a church plant, will have anxious moments; this can be risky business.

So we embrace the challenges of this day. Plan a vacation, take your partner on a date, watch a good movie. Then, return to your assignment with a clear head. We accept that there are easier paths we have chosen not to travel. We move forward, utterly dependent upon Jesus. We do this all to follow him into the adventure of mission, where there are no guarantees but that he goes with us. One day, there will be affirmation from the Master; but until then, we will risk as Jesus did when he loved greatly. We will plant like Jesus.

Reflect: What feels most "risky" right now in your kingdom work? Where might you reasonably reduce some of that risk, and where must you accept it as part of the adventure?

How are you appropriately managing your anxiety around that risk?

Prayer: *God, I acknowledge today that a more secure place can look very desirable at times. Help me to do my part in the many unknowns of my ministry and embrace those things that are beyond my control, believing that this is the adventure of faith you have for me. Amen.*

❈ 47 ❈

PRAYING FORWARD

Read Luke 10:1-9.

"Ask the Lord of the harvest, therefore, to send out workers into his harvest field."

—Luke 10:2

If you are at all like me, it is really hard to sit still and make significant time for prayer when you have a to-do list as long as your arm to complete before dinnertime. It just feels like I am spinning my wheels while the day is flying by. Pioneering leaders may tend to think that way. We prefer action. When Jesus sent out the seventy-two, we can totally get behind his example of missional engagement as he connected people to the transformational reality of the kingdom. Picture Jesus with people on the margins. That part makes total sense. The first step in the process, however, the part that requires us to slow down and deeply acknowledge our dependency upon God—that can be hard to prioritize. *That long list of tasks will not get done by itself,* we say to ourselves, and so the bias to act now and pray later kicks in.

When Jesus sends out the seventy-two, he first instructs them to "ask the Lord of the harvest, therefore, to send out workers into his harvest field" (Luke 10:2). Jesus' first followers were to first pray and, specifically, to pray for a fresh wave of kingdom workers (see Luke 10:9). It is interesting that Jesus does not pray for kingdom workers from the reserves; there really were no personnel reserves—no sponsoring denomination or parenting church—for the infant kingdom movement to draw from. Rather,

Jesus envisions the kingdom worker resources to be found in the very harvest into which he is directing them. Think about it: He is instructing them, by means of prayer, to build the bridge into God's reign *while they are crossing it*. What could this look like? Is this even possible?

I once visited with Steve, national director for church planting with a large planting agency, who tested this Jesus model for evangelism and community engagement. He expected all of his planters (several hundred per year) to develop at least 1,000 community relationships, capturing names and contact information, before they launched public worship. He then asked a significant portion of those planters to systematically pray for their community contacts, thirty minutes every day, name by name, asking God to bless them and to call them into ministry. After several years of testing this practice, he observed indeed that planters who prayed for laborers for the harvest *from* the harvest did launch stronger and grew faster. Sit with that!

Of course, correlation is not always proof of causation, but this practice is worth pondering. Those daily reviews of contact names in prayer may have strengthened the planters' capacity to recall names and thereby build relationships when they saw those contacts in the marketplace. Perhaps the planters' genuine message of "I prayed for you this week" struck people in a way that awakened their spiritual desire, leading to involvement. Perhaps God directly answered a persistent planter's prayers for partners and leaders. Steve would say that his field test persuaded him that God had, indeed, answered prayers. Whether the reason is human or divine, the recommendation is to pray first.

Of this we can be certain: The ultimate source of workers for the great kingdom movement of God has always come from the harvest. New people and new resources from the harvest engaging as co-laborers in the mission of Jesus have always been the most abundant source for the advancing kingdom, so Jesus instructs us to pray into that. He wisely challenges us to "open [our] eyes and look at the fields," for "they are ripe for harvest" (John 4:35); and prayer is the lens he wants us to use in that vision. The way forward begins with Jesus in prayer.

The to-do list we have as planters is often overwhelming. By nature, planters are action-oriented people who like to be doing things. Jesus calls us off of our feet, however, and onto our knees. He wants us to pray for partners and fellow laborers. He wants us look not backward to the Christian community that sent us but forward into the harvest. In the harvest is where he will meet us with new workers, resources, and partnerships.

He asks us to begin with prayer. He advises that we put prayer first on the list. He will meet us in that quiet place when we plant as he did.

Reflect: What is your spirit saying to you about prayer? Are you trying to muscle your way forward in your ministry when you should be *praying your way forward*? What might you need to do to make prayer integral to planting?

Prayer: *Lord Jesus, I pray for gospel partners yet unseen. In this season of many unknowns, I trust in your kingdom Way as the Lord of the harvest. I trust that you have partners I have yet to discover who will be coworkers. This is your church, and I long to see your provision. Amen.*

☙ 48 ☙

GENERATIVITY

Read John 14:12-14; 2 Timothy 2:2.

> *"Whoever believes in me will do the works I have been doing, and they will do even greater things than these, because I am going to the Father."*

—John 14:12

Developmental psychologist Erik Erikson has identified generativity as a quality that tends to come to us in our more mature years. We are generative, he says, when we are secure enough with our place in the world that we can shift our ambitions and concern toward those who are younger or less developed, in hopes that they would thrive and succeed.[1] It is a mature perspective that most of us reach a bit later than maybe we should. The inner quality of generativity can perhaps help us see the leadership development vision of Jesus and of Paul.

In John 14, Jesus makes a remarkable statement: "Whoever believes in me will do the works I have been doing, and they will do even greater things than these, because I am going to the Father" (v. 12). In this text, our Lord takes us into his vision for the future, in which he sees remarkable gospel progress far in excess of its modest beginnings. He is able to see beyond the bumbling missteps of his disciples, who tend to be tripped up by their own doubts and lagging understanding. More than simply correcting them, Jesus demonstrates generativity when he trains them and gives them a vision for their own effectiveness in kingdom work.

In 2 Timothy 2:2, Paul takes the quality of generativity and explains to Timothy, a young church planter in Ephesus, how it can create a forward multiplying momentum. Second Timothy 2:2 has buried within it four successive leadership transmissions. Paul first identifies himself as having received the gospel from many witnesses, which he, in turn, passes on to Timothy. Timothy, then, is to take that same message and teach faithful people who will be qualified at some future point to teach yet others. Paul does not describe the breadth of impact from that series of transmissions, as Jesus does in John 14 by referring to "greater things" (v. 12). Paul does, however, describe the legacy of one generation sharing with the next, and so on, like seeds scattered by the wind.

Church planters should be generative multipliers in a manner similar to that which Jesus and Paul described. We have to believe that the next disciple could be that next person with whom we connect at a social meet-up. We have to believe that the next key leader could be that next person we meet with for Bible study on Tuesday mornings. We have to believe the next church planter could be the next key leader we take under our wing and mentor to lead a small group. We have to believe that basic human potential, when fused with the Holy Spirit, can yield remarkable kingdom expansion. Kierkegaard says it this way: "Life can be understood looking backwards but must be lived looking forward."[2] It is almost always easier to see leadership succession looking back; we see the unlikely pathway into effectiveness best in retrospect. It is most always harder to see the next leader in advance. But we must believe that as the faith has come to us, so it will be transmitted to the next generation, such that they will likely eclipse our best efforts. We all stand upon the shoulders of others and, by grace, achieve "greater things."

For many years now, I have worked as a church-planting leader for a denomination. I could not begin to tell you the number of times I have recruited a planter with skills far stronger than I had at their stage of the journey. If I let that thought grow, I could become envious or discontent in my current role and restless to plant again. These lessons from Jesus and Paul, however, center my thoughts in the wisdom of generativity. You and I can take genuine joy in others we see who may seem to be surpassing us in their effectiveness. They are proving the words of Jesus to be true.

I once heard someone say, "Never do ministry alone." By this, the advisor was saying that we should always be teaching someone else to do what we are doing as though we were working ourselves out of a job. Think of Jesus taking his disciples with him, showing them how to serve, teach, and lead. He did this because he could see beyond himself and into the future of God's mission. We do that best when we lead from a place of great security in who we are as participants in God's ever-expanding kingdom. We are never diminished when we develop someone else who may have gifts beyond ours. Our impact is never lessened when we mentor someone else who is younger and who has more natural gifting than we have. We are, rather, following in the example of Jesus, who saw down through the ages the "greater things" that were yet to come. That generative quality in our relationship with others is a part of planting like Jesus.

Reflect: What is God saying to you about your own emotional security and the need to raise up and release others into ministry? What might you need to delegate and to whom? Who is the next person you can mentor into ministry and leadership?

Prayer: *Lord Jesus, as you multiplied your impact raising up disciples, teach me to be a multiplier. Help me to know deep security in you, such that I know the joy of raising up and releasing others in your service. I pray in Jesus' name. Amen.*

❈ 49 ❈

THE SECRET STRUGGLE

Read Mark 9:14-29; I Timothy 6:11-16.

> *"Everything is possible for one who believes." Immediately the boy's father exclaimed, "I do believe; help me overcome my unbelief!"*
>
> —Mark 9:23-24

Church planting is a thousand tests of faith. It's a test of faith every day that we venture out to engage our community to believe that the Spirit of God is ahead of us. It is a test of faith to believe that new people will authentically embrace Jesus as we have. It is a test of faith that we will find the leaders who will emerge to share in our vision. It is a test of faith that a zillion details will come together and that a location for worship, which we need and can hardly afford, will be found in time for a launch. Go deeper, and the test of faith sounds something like this: *Am I really called to this? Do I really have the gifts needed? Are there really receptive people in my community? Is this really possible, considering that last person who deserted our team?* Our test of faith is often an inner dialogue between shades of doubt and shades of belief. It is often a silent and secret struggle: *Is God really in this?*

Abraham, the father of faith, faced this struggle and failed often. We should remember that while his faith journey began impressively (see Genesis 12; imagine pulling up stakes and packing your moving van with no particular destination in mind), he had plenty of spiritual failures. It is not until later in his life that he trusts God so fully that he is prepared

to do what seems unthinkable with his son Isaac (see Genesis 22). Abraham's example earns him a special place in the story of redemption. That
belief in what is not seen is the quality that ties the saints of the New Testament and the Old Testament together (see Hebrews 11). It is what God
desires above all, even when it is imperfect: "I believe; help my unbelief!"
(Mark 9:24, NRSV).

The apostle Paul knew the priority of faith both from the Hebrew
scriptures as well as from the stories of Jesus. He undoubtedly knew how
Jesus had marveled at the faith of a Roman centurion (see Luke 7:1-10),
how Jesus had challenged his disciples to show faith in his command over
a storm (see Matthew 8:23-27), or how Jesus had called upon his followers, "Don't let your hearts be troubled. Trust in God, and trust also in
me" (John 14:1, NLT). Knowing these essential teachings of Christ, Paul
challenges Timothy to trust God despite great adversity. The Greek city of
Ephesus, where Timothy was church planting, was home to the temple of
Artemis, which promoted pagan worship and earned a reputation as one
of the Seven Wonders of the Ancient World. Picture Timothy planting a
church in the shadow of one of our thriving commercial business districts
that seems content to ignore spiritual realities. In that space, Paul had a
specific challenge for Timothy.

Twice, Paul makes reference to the struggle to maintain a heart of
faith. In one case, he says, "Fight the good fight of the faith" (1 Tim. 6:12).
From the context, we can tell that he is not talking about a crusade of
outward religious conquest but rather a secret inner battle to trust God
(see v. 11). In the second case, Paul speaks autobiographically, saying, "I
have fought the good fight, I have finished the race, I have kept the faith"
(2 Tim. 4:7). Again, he is referencing an inner striving over the length of
his years, like that of a distance runner, to keep believing, day after day. In
these verses, Paul is using the language of a conflict, a battle, a struggle to
believe. It's as if Paul is saying there is a profound inner tension that goes
with ministry, and especially with pioneer planting.

A planter I know acknowledged that they can become secretly cynical
at times. This cynicism slipped out in public now and then, which means
it probably flowed liberally at home. Cynicism is a kind of negativity of the
spirit. It can become chronic pessimism, and it usually evolves as a way

to manage disappointment. For those of us who slip into it, we know it begins with an inner dialogue that can be joined by other cynical voices. Therefore, we too must fight like Timothy. Beware the company of too many cynics!

Fighting the good fight of faith is, at the core, a persistent commitment to believe that Jesus has a good outcome for us. To keep that faith requires that we feed it with the promises and patterns of Jesus over the long haul and hang out with people who are in the same fight. It requires that we attend to our hearts and private thoughts. The kingdom of our Lord will prevail. God is at work for our good, despite circumstances. This is good news when we plant like Jesus.

Reflect: What are the factors that most often poke at your trust in the good future Jesus has for you? What might you need to do in your struggle for an attitude of faith as opposed to one of cynicism? How might you need to feed your soul?

Prayer: *Lord, I feel the challenge to trust that you gave to your disciples. My heart can waver when progress is slow and when adversity comes. Help me to feed my soul in ways that you provide. Thank you that you understand my doubtful days because I pray in Jesus' name. Amen.*

❈ 50 ❈

LEAD YOURSELF

Read Luke 2:52.

> *Jesus matured, growing up in both body and spirit, blessed by both God and people.*
>
> —Luke 2:52, The Message

Perhaps you have heard the advice, "Before you can lead others, you must first show that you can lead yourself." To do that, most of us will turn to various self-management tools, like making a daily to-do list, keeping a personal calendar, budgeting time, and the personal disciplines of punctuality and careful work. These are all very important, but they may obscure the way Jesus modeled self-leadership. Consider all that is packed into Luke 2:52: "Jesus increased in wisdom and in years, and in divine and human favor" (NRSV). The basic teaching of the text was that Jesus grew and that his growth could be measured in at least four dimensions. Let's look for a minute into each of these four areas of Luke 2:52 and consider what they might mean for us as an essential part of our work as start-up pioneers.

First, Jesus grew "in wisdom." We know Jesus was a student of the scriptures and likely also a student of his carpentry craft. For many of us, our craft might be described as leadership, along with theology and ministry. Some of us are in the marketplace bi-vocationally, as Paul was both a planter and a tentmaker (see Acts 18:3), which requires that we grow in another skill set. Following the example of Jesus, we can reasonably ask ourselves the following: *What am I learning lately? What sources am I tapping into to deepen or broaden my understanding? How am I disciplining myself to be a lifelong learner?* The best leaders tend to attribute much of their success to reading consistently and widely. How systematic are we about maturing mentally?

Second, Jesus grew "in years." Physical health can be neglected, and in time, it shows. Jesus seemed to have remarkable stamina for travel and for a ministry that became more demanding over time. There is every indication that he prepared himself for those pressures. See Jesus getting his daily steps in as he moves from town to town! We can reasonably ask ourselves these questions: *Am I getting enough rest? How is my energy level? Do I practice vigorous exercise regularly along with healthy eating habits? What might I need to do to improve in this area?* The mind-body connection is well established in the fields of science. How we treat our bodies impacts our mental and emotional status. Are we attentive to our bodies?

Third, Jesus grew "in human favor." Much of ministry is about relationships. Jesus had a remarkable capacity to develop warm, strong, and purposeful connections with a wide variety of people. While his exchanges with the religious professionals of his day could be frosty, he formed warm connections with people in the marketplace (think of the fishing laborers of Galilee and Zacchaeus) and those on the margins (think of the ten people with leprosy and the widow of Nain). Picture Jesus being a regular member of a service organization or a volunteer chaplain at the local hospital. He could be fully present to an individual or winsome to a crowd. We can reasonably ask ourselves these questions: *How are my relationships in my home, neighborhood, community, and workplace? What might I need to do to develop these? How am I growing in my capacity for redemptive relationships with people in a wide range of spiritual places?*

Finally, Jesus grew "in divine favor." The biblical pictures of Jesus retreating from his work to be with God are frequent. That practice is as essential for those of us who are in professional ministry as it is for those who are not; Jesus proves it to be true. Today, we speak of "spiritual disciplines" as those practices that condition the soul for spiritual effectiveness. Most of those disciplines (solitude, study, fasting, prayer, simplicity, community, generosity), we trace to Jesus' example. We can reasonably ask ourselves the following questions: *Am I deeply connected to God in and through spiritual disciplines? Am I quiet enough before God so that I can hear what I must? What is it that I am hearing when I am alone with Jesus?*

Leading ourselves is a simple and profound part of planting like Jesus. Many of us must be especially intentional to lead ourselves in a balanced way. We all tend to accent a few areas, which may lead to neglect of others. Sometimes, that lopsided style is about a compulsion not to be mediocre in one area. We might even permit ourselves to neglect another area because "it's just not me." The picture we get of Jesus, however, is holistic. He brings his whole self to the mission of God. Over the long haul, leading ourselves in each dimension, as he did, is good for us, good for those we love, and good for the work we seek to advance. Once again, the pattern of Jesus is our model.

Reflect: How does Luke 2:52 challenge you to lead yourself more intentionally? Where might you need to focus for more maturity in self-leadership? What might you be overly invested in at the expense of a balanced life? What intentional steps must you take?

Prayer: *Thank you, Jesus, for your powerful example of self-leadership. I hear the voice of your Spirit through this simple text and desire to take new steps of discipleship. Fill me with your Spirit and grow me into the image of Christ. Amen.*

— 51 —

AUTHENTIC DEMONSTRATION

Read John 13:1-16; 1 Corinthians 11:1.

> *"I have set you an example that you should do as I have done for you. Very truly I tell you, no servant is greater than his master, nor is a messenger greater than the one who sent him."*
>
> —John 13:15-16

Perhaps you have heard a saying related to raising children, "More is caught than taught." Little eyes and ears absorb a great deal from their environment. Jesus seems to recognize that making disciples relies significantly upon the power of his example. "I have set you an example," he says, as he washes their feet (John 13:15). That example of servant leadership is one of the most direct occasions where Jesus names his practice as a pattern for us. On this occasion, as in others, Jesus is authentic and unpretentious. He does not ask us to do what he does not do himself. He is, in this way, a perfect example both in what he does and in how he draws us into kingdom practices.

Church planter and apostle Paul took that example as his own when he said, "Be imitators of me, as I am of Christ" (1 Cor. 11:1, NRSV). The practice of modeling is ideal for church planters, who must develop new people who are not interested in just being religious. More than a psychological factor in child development, modeling is a way we can guide people into an authentic journey with Christ. Let's consider three ways we can reflect the example of Jesus to others, in addition to his servant leadership style.

First, the Gospel writers identify Jesus' habit of prayer more than twenty times.[1] Add to this the fact that Jesus explicitly taught his disciples how to pray, and we must conclude that his example for us in prayer is one we should reflect forward to others (see Luke 11:1-4). Here is an area in which many new followers of Jesus struggle to learn and practice apart from someone's showing them. What does prayer sound like without "churchy" language? Providing an environment for simple sentence prayers or silent guided prayer can help. Without some modeling, such as seeing Jesus do it and teach it, the first disciples would not have learned to pray.

Another area where Jesus was very intentional to show his early followers relates to engaging scripture. It is interesting to note that Jesus quotes the scripture just over sixty times with his disciples.[2] In that modeling, he revealed to them how the text was formative to faith and how it is even worth putting to memory. For Jesus, abiding in the Word—his Word—is essential to being his disciple (see John 15:7). Internalizing scripture is, for us, a further way we show others how to deeply take in the principles of the kingdom.

The greatest area where Jesus was intentional in modeling for his early followers relates to how he drew new people to himself and how he loved deeply: "This is my commandment, that you love one another as I have loved you" (John 15:12, NRSV). He showed his disciples how he loved and related to all types of people and that none should be excluded. He also showed them how using memorable stories and illustrations made his teaching stick. The ministry methods of Jesus were likely ones his disciples practiced when they found themselves leading others.

"I do, we do, you do" is a training sequence used across industries to promote the gradual release of responsibility through modeling and reflection. "I do; you watch" leads to "We do together" leads to "You do; I watch." Each step of the sequence is followed by evaluation and coaching.[3] The success of this simple training sequence says a lot about how effective modeling can be in discipleship. Showing people how to follow Jesus is a tall order. We fail often and fall short. Still, there remains the truth that for most people, "more is caught than taught." Being conscious of our modeling the character and practices of Jesus is part of making new disciples.

We hope that those we develop will learn something about how to handle the ups and downs of life from how *we* handle them. We hope they will learn something about practicing unconditional love from how we embrace the unlovely. We hope they will learn something of how to genuinely seek the kingdom from how we go about our daily lives. Authentic practices are a significant way we plant like Jesus.

Reflect: How conscious are you of the influence of your example to others? Where might you need to be more intentional in modeling to develop others? With whom might you engage in the "I do, we do, you do" method?

Prayer: *Jesus, I am so aware of my weakness and your perfect example. Receive my imperfect efforts to show others your way. Help me to grow in being an example by which others can see a reflection of you and the way of life you want for them, I pray. Amen.*

— 52 —

THIN SKIN

Read Matthew 25:31-46.

> *"'Truly I tell you, whatever you did not do for one of the least of these, you did not do for me.'"*

—Matthew 25:45

There are some jobs that probably require a thick skin. Imagine a stand-up comic who loses his nerve with a tough crowd or a head coach who loses her cool when critiqued in a failing season. We would say they need to learn to let the negativity bounce off them a bit more, like a rubber ball bouncing off a concrete wall. Thicker skin can help us all, sometimes. Our work will not be without critics and Monday-morning quarterbacks.

Many would say, however, that empathy—call it having a thinner skin—is what is in short supply today. Reading the words of Jesus, perhaps empathy is always in danger of being scarce. This is also true for planting leaders. Like anyone else, we can be focused upon our goals and miss picking up on hints coming from an individual with a desperate need. If so, Jesus has a word for us.

In the parable of the sheep and the goats, our Lord paints a picture of the Final Judgment. That may feel like a tough opener; but from Jesus' perspective, the God who will one day make right all the brokenness of the world is also the God who wants to offer abundant life today. If there were no future accountability, then there would be no genuine intent by God for a truly good life in this world. Abundant life would just be nice talk. The point Jesus wants to make in the parable of the sheep and the goats is that part of that design for living involves empathy, the capacity to identify with "the least of these." Let's think, for a bit, about empathy and planting.

While *sympathy* is a feeling of pity or sorrow for someone else, *empathy* takes that feeling a step further. Empathy puts me in your shoes. Empathy makes a deep connection with the plight of the poor, the imprisoned, the hungry, or the homeless. This quality is not taken for granted by Jesus, and for good reason. He had seen a culture lacking empathy and so has strong words for the religious leaders who put heavy religious burdens upon the backs of people or who take issue with his healing on the sabbath. This is worth pausing to consider, as some would say that our culture is seeing a steady loss of empathy as we are able to select our news feed, define our relationships generationally, and gate our neighborhoods. We can virtually shut out the uncomfortable reality of others. Furthermore, studies have shown that the more influential we become, the less empathetic we tend to feel toward those who are in lesser circumstances. We have an ideal environment for thick skin.

Rich was a pastor whose adopted son had made some poor choices, landing him in the Michigan prison system. It was a devastating reality that their family had to accept. That experience, however, led to a spiritual awakening in the son's life, which was an encouragement to Rich. In time, however, his son shared with Rich and other spiritual mentors the challenge of following Christ in prison: It was a virtual spiritual desert behind the prison walls.

Rich heard this with more than a sympathetic ear. He took the next step and deeply empathized with his son's predicament. He put himself in the shoes of his son and others who are incarcerated. Working together, father and son initiated an effort to start a church behind the walls that was more than a ministry to inmates; it was a ministry *with* them. Empathy does that. Empathy forges a deep bond of connection between distant people. As a result, Celebration Church emerged at Ionia State Penitentiary; and in time, dozens of inmates found and formed a spiritual community to support their walk with Jesus.

Empathy connects us deeply with the real predicaments of people. It may even plant a church. Leaders rise in their effectiveness when they are able to identify deeply with others. Jesus calls us to extend that connection to those who are the very least and last, for in so doing, we serve our Lord himself. We also add a dimension to our planting work that grounds us more authentically in the kingdom Jesus came to announce.

Having thin skin is part of planting like Jesus.

Reflect: How open is my heart to the plight of those who are on the margins? How might my circumstances allow me to hide from those in desperate need around me? Where could I make a genuine connection with the last, the least, and the lost?

Prayer: *Jesus, I confess that it is easy to maintain a distance from some people. Help me open my heart to those around me who are unlike me. Show me where my sympathy may need to go further into empathy for those you love. Amen.*

❊ 53 ❊

SOLITARY SPACE

Read Mark 1:35-39; Luke 5:16.

> *But Jesus himself would often slip away to the wilderness
> and pray.*
>
> —Luke 5:16, NASB

From my observation over the years, church planters as a group are relational people. They tend to see a stranger as just another friend they
have not met yet. That attraction to people is an essential quality and
behavior that predicts success. One of the ways that quality shows up
is in the way we recharge our batteries, which could be a night out with
friends. For many of us, people give us energy. While all that human
connection is a good thing, there are practices that may be a bit counterintuitive yet have profound potential to form us deeply in the character
of Jesus. One such practice is how our Lord demonstrates an unavoidable
rhythm of "solitary space." There is evidence to say that this was more
than an occasional experience for Jesus. He seems to be very deliberate
about his alone time. Let's look again at some of references that seem
almost peripheral at first, until you add them all up.

There are a great many references to the prayer life of Jesus, and a
significant number of those describe this practice for him as a solitary
experience. Examples include, "He went up on the mountain by himself
to pray" (Matt. 14:23, RSV); "Jesus himself would often slip away to the
wilderness and pray" (Luke 5:16, NASB); "He left them again, and went
away and prayed" (Matt. 26:44, NASB). Being alone with God in prayer

regularly appears to be Jesus' habit. In Mark 1:35, we get a picture of that practice that is worth pondering further: Jesus rises early, "while it was still dark." Being deeply connected to God is the first priority of the day for him. It happens before other demands crowd in—before he "checks his email and social networks." While this text may not be prescribing that we all be early-morning people, it does show us how Jesus made time with God an essential part of his day. This is not always easy, especially in our time, and especially with personal electronic devices and home-officing.

Next comes the reference to a "solitary place" (Mark 1:35). Jesus knew where to go so that he would not be disturbed in his time with God. For him, that was increasingly a challenge as he became more popular. For us, that is a challenge as well, as we have portable devices that keep us connected with notifications at every turn. Many of us may do our work at a coffee shop and do not have a dedicated office space. Like Susanna Wesley, who was surrounded by her children, we may have to throw our aprons up over our heads to somehow shut out the many distractions and be alone with God.[1]

Finally, there is evidence from the Gospels that solitary prayer gave Jesus true insight into future plans in his ministry. He emerges from his time away with urgency to move on to new villages where he would minister.

Nate and Keith were planting as a team and found that they were able to maintain a rhythm of early-morning prayer, rising before dawn, by sharing that commitment together. They would alternate who was interceding morning by morning. Alone, they might not have been as successful in maintaining the practice over time; but together, they kept it up. Amy, another planter, shared how she would go for her regular cardio run and "pray without ceasing" (1 Thess. 5:17, NRSV) as she pounded the pavement. For her, that was the habit she could maintain. Yet another planting friend, Rob, recommended to fellow start-up pioneers a spiritual retreat center where he would go once a month for a day away to pray and listen to God speak. In that space, he could totally unplug for a day away with Jesus. Oftentimes, he would join in the rhythms of prayer established by the Christian community resident within that place. It gave him a structure to guide his alone time.

What is clear from the example of each of these highly entrepreneurial and effective leaders is that they found a method that fit their personal style to maintain the practice of solitude and the priority of a rhythm of prayer. It is not hard to draw a connection between the ministry impact of Jesus and his regular times in private intercession. Picture Jesus alone with God in the garden of Gethsemane, as he both pours out his heart and steels his resolve to be fully obedient to the will of the One who sent him.

Locating solitary space may take some discipline to jump-start. In time, we are likely to agree with our Lord Jesus and many others who have come to find that time as being essential for spiritual power in kingdom-building work.

Reflect: How is God calling you into deeper connection through regular prayer? How might you find solitary space in your life for time alone with God? What is unique about your schedule that can help you design time for solitude and prayer?

Prayer: *God of life and love, I hear you calling me into relationship with you. Teach me to pray and seek solitude as Jesus did. As I seek to come near to you, come close to me and reveal yourself to me, I pray. Amen.*

⚜ 54 ⚜

STAY HUMBLE

Read Luke 9:46-50; 14:11.

"All those who exalt themselves will be humbled, and those who humble themselves will be exalted."

—Luke 14:11

It is not uncommon for spiritual entrepreneurs to have a healthy dose of what some have referred to as "benign narcissism." Call it ego strength or healthy self-confidence, apostolic work can benefit from some appropriate chutzpah. Most of us need a shot of inner motivation deriving from confident certainty that we are called to this work by God: With the Holy Spirit's help, we can do this!

However, in his book *When Narcissism Comes to Church: Healing Your Community from Emotional and Spiritual Abuse*, Chuck DeGroat reminds us of how damaging our pride can be. While we all are susceptible to narcissistic behavior and feelings of superiority, a deeper, more serious disorder is characterized by grandiosity, entitlement, a need for admiration, and a lack of empathy. Those who tend toward this unhealthy orientation may be charming and inspiring to others, but too much has become a mask for what is truly inside. DeGroat goes on to describe how narcissism can thrive among Christians who see themselves as being uniquely used or blessed by God and who can compare themselves to others in ministry who appear inferior.[1]

The disciples may have had some of that same narcissism when they had an argument among themselves about who would be the greatest. In that situation, found in Luke 9, Jesus let them down gently by placing a child within their midst while teaching them that in the kingdom, greatness is not measured as they would expect it to be: "It is the one who is least among you all who is the greatest" (v. 48). We might think that was a memorable-enough illustration to make the point. Still, their egos are unbridled as John speaks up: "We saw someone casting out demons in Your name; and we tried to prevent him because he does not follow along with us" (v. 49, NASB). We cannot be certain exactly who it was that John had spotted. We know that Jesus had sent out others and, at one point, had commissioned seventy-two disciples to go out declaring and demonstrating the kingdom; perhaps those casting out demons in Luke 9 were other witnesses he had sent out. What we can be certain of is the smallness of mind the disciples exhibited when they tattled to Jesus about another kingdom worker who did not quite line up with their practices. Tribal thinking had them in an "us and them" mentality. In Jesus' mind, that other kingdom worker evidently was making a valuable contribution despite their objections: "Do not stop him, for whoever is not against you is for you" (Luke 9:50). In this correction, Jesus calls them out of their narrow sense of identity ("he does not follow along with us") and into a larger vision of his kingdom community.

One of the best things you and I can do from time to time is to get out of our little envelopes of comfort and security that tend to go with whatever identity group we are part of and step into another environment that makes us feel small. Dave is a planter who was challenged to do just that by his coach. The coach suggested to Dave, who was planting in a mainline tradition, that he should visit the fastest-growing church in his community, which happened to be nondenominational. That is actually a fairly smart suggestion, given that many of the fastest- and largest-growing churches today are not denominational churches. Admittedly, it took Dave a while to get past his denominational defensiveness and a somewhat critical attitude and actually see the effective methods that another church had developed. Some of these deeply challenged practices that Dave traced back to his seminary education. To his credit, he listened and learned. Eventually, Dave swallowed his pride and adopted some of those methods, and he saw some good results.

Terri is another planter who joined a cohort of leaders from other denominations in order to learn from them. She was smart enough to recognize that her people did not have all the answers. Terri grew more quickly through that exposure. Both Dave and Terri discovered valuable things when they were willing to humble themselves a bit.

Church planting tends to break down our pride eventually, whether we like it or not. It breaks down some of our ego and some of our misplaced identity. Because we are first and foremost about the kingdom, our church identities and any pride of position should melt away. We can let that humbling take place down the road someday and postpone the benefit of learning from and participating with others. A better option, though, is to see Jesus putting a child in the midst of us today, while saying, "The one who is least among you is the one who will be the greatest" (Luke 9:48, adapted).

Humility tends to open us up to the greater wisdom Jesus has for us. This change of heart and mind is essential to planting like Jesus.

Reflect: How might others judge your level of humility? How many friends do you have outside of your "crew"? What indicators are there that you are willing to be like a child, so that you might receive the wisdom Jesus has for you?

Prayer: *Lord, I confess that I too am like the disciples, foolishly taken in by my own "greatness" and dismissive of others you want me to learn from. Help me to see the greatness found in humility, and teach me today, for Jesus' sake. Amen.*

❖ 55 ❖

INTERGENERATIONAL ENGAGEMENT

Read Matthew 18:2-5; 19:13-14.

> *"Truly I tell you, unless you change and become like little children, you will never enter the kingdom of heaven."*
>
> —Matthew 18:3

Way too often, children's ministry is considered a bit of a chore in start-up work. First, you need to have the required space. Then, there are all the cribs and toys and changing tables and the age-appropriate educational stuff. Then it really gets chaotic, with endless volunteer recruitment (and volunteer burnout) and those essential background checks. Little wonder that this area is sometimes considered the caboose on the planting train. Jesus, on the other hand, sees potential in children that may be worth reconsidering.

The Jewish culture of Jesus' day had a pattern of having children brought to the elders on the evening of the Day of Atonement to receive a blessing. It was a significant event that brought out the whole family to celebrate, and we might imagine aunts and uncles and others among the gathering of happy family. The event in Matthew 19 may very well have been that type of occasion. The spontaneous activity of parents bringing these little ones to Jesus likely caught the disciples off guard. They felt that Jesus had more important things to be occupied with, and thus their rebuke. But Jesus connects with the children, welcomes them, and makes himself fully available to them. Then, he speaks words of affirmation: The kingdom belongs to those who are like children.

This is the second time Jesus makes this point, as if for emphasis. Earlier, in Matthew 18, it was said, "[Jesus] called a little child to him, and placed the child among them. And he said: 'Truly I tell you, unless you change and become like little children, you will never enter the kingdom of heaven. Therefore, whoever takes the lowly position of this child is the greatest in the kingdom of heaven. And whoever welcomes one such child in my name welcomes me.'" (vv. 2-5).

What Jesus is teaching is that in the kingdom, the value scale is the opposite from what we typically think. Children are intrinsically valued and can have a significant impact upon others. They both model faith and draw others to that modeling. Who can argue with the affection Jesus has for these little ones? What we may not always appreciate is the potential children have to engage adults in their own faith formation. A number of innovative planting strategies like Messy Church emphasize intergenerational worship and thereby leverage this principle.[1] Some congregations intentionally set up a quiet (or, in some cases, not-so-quiet) play area in the general worship space to promote this same principle. When we engage kids with Jesus, we can draw adults toward Jesus.

Tim and Anna are the children of parents who had walked out of church soon after they were married. For nearly two decades, Mom and Dad had hardly darkened a church door except for an occasional funeral or wedding. One day, Tim and Anna got invited to attend a youth group event at a local church. That experience left those siblings wanting more. In time, they began asking their parents to came along to worship. Years later, these two parents are among the most-invested regular attenders of a local congregation. Those children inadvertently drew their de-churched parents' attention to Jesus.

Kids have a big effect on others, but there is more to consider here for start-up leaders. Children's ministry sometimes can be considered a necessary-but-challenging appendage of church planting: "If we could just 'farm it out' to a video screen and a rotation of volunteers, we'd be covered." But when Jesus says, "To such belongs the kingdom of heaven" (Matt. 19:14, rsv), he is including with the children all who may feel their lives are insignificant or peripheral. That includes those who are unemployed, those who are service-industry workers, those who are chronically ill, and those who are otherwise marginalized. When the children are valued and celebrated for who they are, as they were by Jesus, many others are made to feel they too have worth in the kingdom.

What we do in our design and development of children's ministry ripples out in many directions, sending a message. Little wonder that many growing churches prominently display and promote their children's programming near the front door. Prioritizing children can help us successfully plant like Jesus.

Reflect: What place does children's ministry have in your planting work? Do you think of the simple faith of children as a blessing? How might you need to further lift up this dimension of your planting work? To whom in children's ministry should you express appreciation?

Prayer: *Lord, thank you for the gift of the children. Forgive me if I have been looking past them and show me how they too have a role in building your kingdom in this place, for Jesus' sake. Amen.*

❄ 56 ❄

RECOVERING BROKEN TRUST

Read Matthew 18:15-17; 2 Timothy 4:9-15.

> *"If your brother or sister sins, go and point out their fault, just between the two of you. If they listen to you, you have won them over."*

—Matthew 18:15

Few things hurt more than a damaged or broken relationship. We may feel we truly know someone, and then they turn from us—or worse, they turn on us. Betrayal, desertion, disloyalty, and sabotage may be somewhat different, but they share in common a shattered trust. Under most any circumstances, it is tough to take. Under the stress and strain of a planting venture, it can feel devastating.

In my own planting experience, I recall a year when several families approached me, all on their own and for different reasons, to indicate that they would no longer be able to participate in the ministry. While their individual reasons for taking a different path made perfect sense to them—and, honestly, I too could see their reasoning—for me it felt like a breach of trust. While they never turned upon me, I felt they had turned *from* me. I now know my discouraging experience is a common one for planters.

Jesus faced broken trust in his relationships. He knew the disappointment of denial with Peter and the sting of betrayal with Judas. The outcomes of those ruptured relationships were certainly not the same. In Matthew 18, he gives his disciples a pattern for handling broken relationships. First, we look at ourselves (see vv. 8-9): What have I contributed to the broken relationship, and how can I take responsibility? If the problem remains, second, go to the person one on one (see v. 15). The idea is not to draw others into the conflict, nor is the idea to directly settle the score. A one-on-one meeting is for seeking reconciliation by understanding the other's point of view. If the problem remains, third, get some objective help (see v. 16), first from an individual and then, if need be, from a faith community (see v. 17). Restoration and recovery are always the preferred outcome.

Paul faced similar relationship struggles with close associates in his mission work. In 2 Timothy 4, there are references to the desertion of Demas (see v. 10) and the outright damaging offense of Alexander (see v. 14). Elsewhere, Paul experienced a falling out with John Mark, who had deserted him at one point in his journey (see Acts 15:37-39). With John Mark, there is evidence of a redemptive outcome, as he paired with Barnabas for a new mission and trust began to be rebuilt. For both Jesus and Paul, the outcomes from broken relationships were mixed; we cannot always control the ending.

Relationships fracture for so many reasons. Tom Nebel and Gary Rohrmayer have written about trust building in church-planting leadership in their book *Church Planting Landmines: Mistakes to Avoid in Years 2 through 10*.[1] They observe two dimensions of trust that have to be solid for an effective partnership. First, they've discovered that partners need to trust the planter's vision. As is sometimes the case, people come from another church with their own ideas of what a new church should be like. Oftentimes, these folks carry a vision as a hangover from past experiences, such that they want us to embrace it. After a season of subtle tension or outright sabotage, we may have to graciously and finally make it clear that we are not exchanging our vision for theirs. Relationships can fracture when visions collide, requiring hard conversations.

And second, according to Nebel and Rohrmayer, people need to trust the planter as a person. As in any new relationship, it takes some time to see the other person's character for what it is. For example, do they always keep their word? Do they tell the unvarnished truth? Are they principled in decision-making? Are their personal ethics honorable? So, we might imagine a case where there is a shared commitment to the vision but not to the leader. We might also imagine a case where there is shared commitment to the leader but not to the vision. In either case, we can see how trust is essential for a strong partnership, and alignment around the vision and the leader are at least two ways to measure that trust.

In the life of Jesus and the early church, there are examples of people who could not commit to the vision, to the leader, or to either one. Facing these losses is not easy. The experience can drain away precious time and emotional energy. Both Jesus and Paul recognized broken trust when it occurred, and they demonstrated a direct communication style that best opened the way for a redemptive outcome. They were then able to move forward on the mission God had given them, confident they had done their best to stay in relationship. This too may be needed, if we are to plant like Jesus.

Reflect: Where do you feel the wounds of broken trust? How are you doing at following the model found in Matthew 18? How are you growing wiser in your leadership through those experiences?

Prayer: *Lord Jesus, you know the pain of disloyalty that I have, and will, experience. Teach me your way of handling conflict. Help me to protect the vision you have given me, as well as to love those who choose another way, I pray. Amen.*

❊ 57 ❊

WOBBLY TRANSITIONS

Read Matthew 14:27; Acts 10:1-48.

"Take courage! It is I. Don't be afraid."

—Matthew 14:27

Change happens—changes of plans, changes of staffing, changes in leadership, changes in direction. I know a church plant that changed locations so often that its people had to go online each Saturday to confirm which school or hotel ballroom or movie theater they would be worshiping in that week. Sometimes, change in our planting work is anticipated, and we are eager to get to it: The ministry is growing, and we are excited to get into a new space. Sometimes, change is not anticipated, and we are faced with temporary chaos. Who among us has not had an amazing support-staff member or volunteer person resign, and then, suddenly, we realize how critical that person was to operations? The thoughts and emotions associated with change can be the hardest reality to manage. Take Peter, for example.

Peter is settled within his Jewish culture when one day, prior to lunch, he retreats at a rooftop restaurant for his ritual prayers. Peter's life is generally predictable inside the Jewish cultural envelope, but that is about to change. It begins with an argument he has with God over food (see Acts 10:9-16). In a dream, not once, not twice, but three times, God tells him to eat freely of any food, to which Peter replies, "Surely not, Lord! I have never eaten anything impure or unclean" (v. 14). That experience stirs up objections inside his head, throwing him off balance; Peter moves from a fairly stable worldview to a "wobbly" one. That is often how transitions begin. Imagine Peter, scratching his head as he tries to match his vivid dream with everything he has assumed to be true. And then, things get really crazy.

Peter is pushed from an unsteady place into a radically unfamiliar space when three unexpected visitors come looking for him, representing Cornelius, a centurion (see Acts 10:17-20). This puts Peter way outside his comfort zone, leading to an unplanned road trip to the home of Cornelius and entry into Roman Gentile military culture. Imagine Peter's mind spinning as he contrasts his former predictable life inside the Jewish bubble with this new, disorienting place in which he finds himself.

We can tell, however, that Peter is moving from this disorienting experience to a new mental and emotional place when he is able to talk openly about this change he is navigating: "God has shown me that I should not call anyone impure or unclean" (Acts 10:28). Imagine Peter, still surprised, as he is listening to the sound of his own voice describing Gentile inclusion. This is Peter's second mentally wobbly experience as he begins to live, little by little, into a new reality. Peter is gradually finding a new voice and a new sense of comfort with the gospel of Jesus, one that embraces Jews and Gentiles alike. By the end of the story, Peter has clearly landed in a new place of mental clarity around the Gentile mission and his Jewish practices. Granted, Peter's change of perspective is a far more profound reality than most of us will ever face. But the process he went through can throw light on our planting shake-ups.

Terry is a planter whose start-up was launched into the unknown when his congregation's worship space was sold out from under them. He knew it was coming when the rent-free building they were in was deemed beyond repair. Working in an urban context, it was a big loss. Finding affordable space would be a huge challenge. Terry had little alternative but to jump on the emotional ride through change that included uncomfortable and chaotic seasons, as they let go of what was known and then eventually entered another challenging phase as they adjusted to a new regular location. Finding their new place has turned out to be a big win, but Terry could not see that at first. It takes considerable time for us to navigate the mental and emotional dimensions of transition.

Peter had more than one experience with Jesus taking him through a significant change of expectations. Walking on water was certainly wobbly and chaotic and likely made a lasting impression (see Matthew 14:25-32)! I imagine Peter remembered that encounter with Jesus on the Sea of Galilee as he came to fully understand his experience on a rooftop in Acts 10. Jesus was stretching Peter's faith in each incident, and Peter grew as a disciple.

Transitions are not easy. The words of Jesus—"Take courage! It is I. Do not be afraid" (Matt. 14:27)—are words we should not forget. The Lord is with us through the unexpected and unnerving episodes as we plant like Jesus.

Reflect: Where are you today in terms of navigating change? What are you feeling? How does the mental and emotional experience of Peter help you understand your own transitions?

Prayer: *Sovereign Lord, while I recognize that you are intent on my good, there are times when my journey does not feel that way. I wonder what you are up to and whether things will ever settle down. Help me trust you, knowing that you are with me and are working for good. Amen.*

⚜ 58 ⚜

COMPARISON IS POISON

Read John 21:15-23.

"What is that to you? You must follow me."

—John 21:22

Planting in a hyperconnected world has its advantages. We can livestream conferences and be inspired by great speakers while we sit behind our garage-sale desk in our home office / bedroom. We can also wander the web and see ministries with far better accommodations than ours. We can follow our friends on Facebook who have larger congregations, larger budgets for fun staff retreats, nicer homes, and who take far better vacations. This is usually when we discover the poison of comparison.

In John 21, Jesus faces off with Peter, reinstating him for future ministry with that memorable, thrice-repeated question, "Do you love me?" (v. 15). Hinting back to Peter's threefold denial of him (referenced in all four Gospels), Jesus comes with a fresh, gracious invitation for Peter to live the kingdom vision by feeding his new followers (John 21:15-17). Jesus' instruction to him to "feed my sheep" (v. 17) communicates great love as Jesus recommissions him, despite his past failure. It seems Peter is headed into a fruitful ministry, from which he will eventually retire and age out as the elder statesman of the early church. But then, the conversation takes an uncomfortable turn.

In verses 18-19, Jesus paints a hard picture for Peter, saying, "When you are old you will stretch out your hands, and someone else will dress you and lead you where you do not want to go." Peter undoubtedly sees in those words a future of great suffering and pain. So, he does what most of us do: He looks for some immediate relief by comparison. "Lord, what about him?" Peter asks, seeing John (v. 21). Peter compares his future to John's because he does not like the path Jesus has indicated for him. If Peter cannot be free of future suffering, he at least wants to be sure that John doesn't get a pass; if John will not suffer, why should he? *This is not fair!*

Comparison is poison to our soul and spirit. Sadly, however, comparing is still what we do. We find someone who is doing worse than we are so that we can feel better for a few minutes. We find someone who is doing better, and we feel miserable and then wallow in it. The fact is, there will always be people doing better than we are; they will have a better building, budget, location, team, and income. Planters are prone to this because often, we choose to start with less—we choose a blank canvas to design and build a new church free of the mistakes of predecessors. Lucky us! But then comes Monday, and we ask, "What about them—those pastors with a staff and an office and a dedicated building? What about them, Lord? I am getting hammered out here, and they have it easy."

To all that frustration, Jesus replies, "What is that to you? You must follow me" (John 21:22). In other words, "Stop comparing yourself with others, Peter! Am I not enough for you?"

Comparison is a mood killer. It stirs up envy, which in turn leaves us feeling lousy. When we compare, we fail to recognize what those whose possessions we lust after have already endured or the present struggle they are slogging through that we may never see. Comparison is also a retreat into loneliness. It says, *I will suffer through this miserable life of mine. Woe is me.* Rather than reaching out to form partnerships with others and making the most of where we are, comparison hides us in misery and cuts us off from relationships in bitterness. Finally, comparison throws cold water on creativity. It takes our spirit of kingdom adventure and drains it away in a waste of time and mental energy. Comparison hijacks the kingdom potential others saw in us when they commissioned us to do pioneer work.

Oftentimes, the disadvantage we may talk ourselves into can be reframed as an advantage if we will just stop comparing. In the past, bivocational planting (my personal experience) was seen as a low rung on the ladder of ministry success. Today, we understand better how that incarnational approach has tremendous advantages for those who have a skill they can leverage. I did not always see that years ago, and I wasted mental energy on comparing myself with others rather than making the most of that marketplace potential. Big mistake. *Big.*

Our kind Savior has a better way for us: "Come and follow me. Take your eyes off of others and fix them completely upon me and my great love for you. My path for you may not be easy, but it is far better than poison." Planting like Jesus includes receiving the assignment God has given us, believing that our Lord understands the difficulty we face today and is with us. Our Lord knows about all our troubles. He has been where we are at. Accepting our place is indeed planting like Jesus.

Reflect: What are the "triggers" that tempt you to compare yourself with others? What can you give thanks for today? Where do you hear Jesus calling to you, "Follow me"?

Prayer: *Thank you, Lord, for this place where I am. Save me from foolish envy and comparison with others. Fill me with your Spirit of creativity and power in the place where you have me, I pray. I receive this day as a gift from you. Amen.*

❈ 59 ❈

RESILIENCE

Read Matthew 16:24; Philippians 3:7-11.

> *I want to know Christ—yes, to know the power of his resur-*
> *rection and participation in his sufferings.*
>
> —Philippians 3:10

We are hardwired for resilience. We have more capability to recover from a setback than we think. New experiences are giving us added insight and wisdom. Expanding relationships are giving us added networks and support. Others are believing in us when we may not be believing in ourselves. The ups and downs of church planting are normal. I know that it may feel like we are peddling a tricycle through quicksand, but the seasons of setback we experience will pass. Rolling with the punches is part of this work. We all are in good company when things are tough. Better days will come—I just know it!

The characters of scripture are no strangers to setbacks. Job, Joseph, and, of course, Jesus: "He came to that which was his own, but his own did not receive him" (John 1:11). Paul faced profound setbacks in his planting work. Some of that struggle is detailed in 2 Corinthians 4, where he states, "We are hard pressed on every side, but not crushed; perplexed, but not in despair" (v. 8). In chapter eleven of the same book, Paul details his experience further: "Three times I was beaten with rods, once I was pelted with stones, three times I was shipwrecked, I spent a night and a day in the open sea" (v. 25). When I am having a bad day, I find that reading that entire chapter has a way of snapping me back into gratitude. How did Paul not sink into mind-numbing cynicism and paralysis, given the physical and emotional bumps and bruises he endured? I will never fully understand, but I have a clue.

I believe that church planter Paul saw in the suffering and resurrection of Jesus a paradigm for his own experience, as Jesus denied himself and took up a cross (see Matthew 16:24). In that service, however, God had not abandoned him, but rather was transforming his struggle into victory. Death gave way to resurrection. Paul speaks of deeply identifying with Jesus in that experience: "I want to know Christ—yes, to know the power of his resurrection and participation in his sufferings, becoming like him in his death" (Phil. 3:10). Elsewhere, he writes of Jesus, "Death is at work in us, but life is at work in you" (2 Cor. 4:12). Paul could see the price he was paying on a personal level, while he also saw the benefit others were receiving. Deeper still, he knew that he was participating in the suffering of Jesus with resurrection hope; knowing this was Paul's lifeline.

Jeb came to Chicago from India to plant a church among the immigrant community in that great city. He was the first of his family to come to the United States, and he struggled with loneliness, having left behind a wife and family, who would come later. Progress was slow, as cultural differences made adjusting difficult. The planting group that he gathered around him was fragile at first, and at times they struggled with disagreements. In the middle of Jeb's epic challenge, he could rely only upon God and upon healthy habits to get him through. So, he put his mind to cultivating a circle of friends, engaging in exercise, observing a personal sabbath, and having patience. Some setbacks, we cannot muscle through quickly. We must find a pace to finish the race. In time, Jeb's wife and family arrived, his planting ministry began to take shape, and Chicago began to feel like a new home. The loneliness lifted; the planting work began to take hold. Resurrection days had come!

In the early church, they knew the resurrection power of Jesus through experience. The book of Acts is, by many accounts, a series of setbacks, each followed by a season of resurrection power. Persecution scattered the church, yet growth was the result (see Acts 5). Internal debate and dissension were resolved, leading to unforeseen expansion (see Acts 15).

The arrest of Paul in Jerusalem led to his opportunity to proclaim Christ in Rome (see Acts 21–28).

Rachel told me of her planting experience when she was blessed with ten volunteers from a church who had come to help her. By the end of her first year, each of those volunteers had left, being unwilling to enter deeply into the vision. It was a low point. In time, however, God sent new leaders who did have the missional outlook needed for success. Resurrection days had come!

Setback was, and is, never final. It is, and has always been, prelude to the advance that God will bring next. This is particularly true for the people of God and those who plant. This is the resurrection hope we carry in our work through the ups and downs. Such confidence is quietly ours when we plant like Jesus.

Reflect: How are you managing yourself through the setbacks you are experiencing? What practices are helping you remain steady under pressure? What is God teaching you through your journey with Jesus?

Prayer: *Lord Jesus, as you suffered for me, so, now, I am learning your way of the cross. Self-denial does not come easy for me. I need your Spirit filling me with inner peace and hope. Thank you that I am in good company with your resurrection people. Amen.*

✸ 60 ✸

STAYING ON MISSION

Read John 20:19-31.

> *Again Jesus said, "Peace be with you! As the Father has sent me, I am sending you."*
>
> —John 20:21

There is a trend in ministry that could be called "evangelism entropy": It is the tendency that overtakes new Jesus communities to turn inward and forget their original purpose. Regrettably, it happens way too often on most every level when Christians organize. Take the history of Methodism, for example. In 1776, about 2 percent of Americans were Methodist. By 1850, about 34 percent of Americans were Methodist.[1] That's remarkable growth, for sure! Equally remarkable is the decline of evangelistic energy and practice in Methodism in the years since 1850. What is true for a movement like Methodism is similarly true for individuals and churches. Evangelistic entropy overtakes us. It even happens to church-planting teams.

In John 20, Jesus walks in on his disciples while they are in a serious season of mission retreat. The Crucifixion has knocked the wind out of their sails, and they are full of fear. They imagine that if the Jewish leaders were to find them, who knows but that they too might be forced to pay with their lives. At least they are together and can experience familiar comfort with comrades. Imagine them taking solace in old friends and past memories. Imagine them nostalgically retelling those favorite episodes with Jesus, over and over, gradually drifting off mission.

Just then, Jesus appears and blesses them with his peace. Their failure to follow him closely through the week of his trial and crucifixion is all forgiven. And then in the same breath, he says to them, "As the Father has sent me, I am sending you" (v. 21). This is not the first time he has sent the disciples with similar words. In John 13, Jesus says, "Very truly I tell you, whoever accepts anyone I send accepts me" (v. 20). In John 17:18, our Lord describes his Incarnation as our example, saying, "As you sent me into the world, I have sent them into the world." When these remarks are paired with the clear teaching of Jesus to "go and make disciples of all nations" in Matthew 28:19, it is clear that Jesus did not want the disciples holed up in a room, veering off-mission. From where we sit, it is easy to diagnose their problem while failing to see our own.

Rob felt his congregation was straying off mission but was struggling with turning things around. Weary of one more new program to fire up evangelistic energy among his group, he decided to work toward calibrating every dimension of the ministry with evangelistic values. Beginning with himself, he signed up for the local evening hockey "Geezer League" and began working on building new relationships with people who avoided church. It felt good to get out of the church bubble and clear his head with a bunch of guys who were trying to fight back the inevitable effects of middle age. Maybe, just maybe, there would come an appropriate time to share his faith in an authentic and natural way.

Meanwhile, Rob tackled the ministry, working to orient every aspect toward an evangelistic outcome, a strategy sometimes called "organic outreach."[2] He evaluated worship to be sure it was designed with a sensitivity to outsiders. Meetings again started with team members sharing whom they were building relationships with in order to share Jesus. Events were designed to be easy to invite friends. His preaching avoided insider jargon. Hospitality, youth, children, small groups, communications and technology—every ministry area was adjusted with a bias toward outreach and evangelism. The whole process has not been easy, as insider preference, assumptions, and language can quickly overtake church culture. In time, however, a new sense of missional purpose found its way back into most every dimension of the church. Evangelism entropy was pushed back, and a fresh culture of community engagement, personal interaction, and corporate witness began to emerge.

Evangelistic entropy becomes harder to turn around as a ministry grows and matures. Addressing the drift early is always the best option. Jesus shows us that priority of staying on mission by virtue of his repeated challenge: "As the Father has sent me, I am sending you." Staying on mission will always be our mandate if we want to plant like Jesus.

Reflect: Are there indications that your ministry has turned inward? What might you need to do to reorient your ministry toward outsiders and missional values? How might you reorient each aspect of your work to be more attentive to the priority of reaching new people?

Prayer: *Lord of the harvest, help me to see where I may have drifted from your purpose for me. Restore to me the joy of my salvation, such that I will follow you in your love for the last, the least, and the lost. Renew me in the practice of living as your sent servant, I pray. Amen.*

Epilogue

"YOUR MISSION, SHOULD YOU DECIDE TO ACCEPT IT"[1]

Read Luke 24:13-27.

Beginning with Moses and all the Prophets, he explained to
them what was said in all the Scriptures concerning himself.

—Luke 24:27

Much of the writing of *Plant Like Jesus* took place in the midst of the great national and international challenges of 2020. It has been quite a remarkable year. A global pandemic and economic recession, racial injustice and the ensuing turmoil, plus mounting concerns with environmental warming, western wildfires, and a national election in the US—a potent brew for concern, if ever there was one. What does Jesus say to us now about these pressing concerns of our day? How do we plant like Jesus when our questions may seem different from those he answered in his earthly ministry?

In Luke 24, Jesus encountered his disciples on the Emmaus road. They too faced a set of circumstances that they had not foreseen, and they were struggling with how to proceed as disciples of the Messiah from Nazareth. In that encounter, Jesus took them into the Hebrew scriptures and opened their eyes to those things pertaining to himself. He directed the disciples to search and find him there.

I believe that Jesus wants to open our eyes to all that the scripture has to say about him and about the perplexing circumstances of our times. To do so, I believe that he would turn us to Genesis as we face global ecological concerns and to the prophets as we face matters of injustice. I believe Jesus would take us to the book of Deuteronomy for insights into how to care for the immigrant and the corporate responsibility we have to speak for those who cannot speak up for themselves. I believe that Jesus has more to show us of himself through the pages of both the Hebrew scriptures and our New Testament. In fact, we can see throughout the epistles how Paul and the other writers build upon the teachings of Jesus to draw out further implications, as many of our devotionals have already shown. In those letters, we can hear the echo of Jesus speaking to us further about our present challenges. Our mission, should we decide to accept it, is to dig deep into those sacred texts to hear from Jesus. In that effort, I believe he will meet us there. To use the words of Jesus, "Seek and you will find" (Matt. 7:7).

As those early disciples walked with Jesus to Emmaus, they found themselves wanting more of him—"they urged him strongly, 'Stay with us'"—and so they shared a meal together wherein Jesus revealed more of himself to them. For us, as we also long for more from Jesus to answer the difficult questions in our planting work and in our community ministries, it will be essential for us to stay with him. He will be present to us by his Spirit, through the witness of scripture, and in the community of believers. He will speak if we stay with him.

The news cycles and talk chatter around us will likely grow louder in coming years. Loud voices want to be heard. God, on the other hand, often speaks quietly; I believe we can say that, in light of the story of Elijah and the "still small voice of God" (see 1 Kings 19:11-13, NRSV). One author calls it "divine shyness."[2] God does not give us all the answers we want, exactly when we want them and at the level of clarity that we want them. We will need to seek regularly and quietly listen.

I believe that as we seek and listen, Jesus will continue to speak to us about how we plant earthly representations of his body and how we message the kingdom of God. My hope is that *Plant Like Jesus* will lead us continually back into that search for many years to come.

NOTES

Chapter 2, First, Listen

1. U2, "Every Breaking Wave," from *Songs of Innocence* (2014).

Chapter 3, Community Engagement

1. W. F. Moulton, A. S. Geden, H. K. Moulton, *Concordance to the Greek Testament* (Edinburgh, Scotland: T. & T. Clark, 1978), 141.

Chapter 4, First Followers

1. "Religious Landscape Study," Pew Research Center website, https://www.pewforum.org/religious-landscape-study.

Chapter 6, Discipling New Followers

1. Harold Rogers, *Harry Denman: A Biography* (Nashville, TN: Upper Room Books, 1977).

Chapter 7, Missional Imagination

1. Rick Richardson, *You Found Me: New Research on How Unchurched Nones, Millennials, and Irreligious Are Surprisingly Open to Christian Faith* (Downers Grove, IL: InterVarsity Press, 2019).
2. "Frequency of Prayer," https://www.pewforum.org/religious-landscape-study/frequency-of-prayer.

Chapter 9, It's All About Relationships

1. Dale Carnegie, *How to Win Friends and Influence People* (New York, NY: Simon and Schuster, Inc.), 1936.

Chapter 11, Jesus' Success Strategy

1. Robert E. Logan, *The Missional Journey: Multiplying Disciples and Churches That Transform the World* (St. Charles, IL: Missional Challenge, 2013).

2. Robert E. Logan, *The Missional Journey: Multiplying Disciples and Churches That Transform the World.*

Chapter 12, Eating and Drinking

1. Susha Roberts, "10 Lessons from Jesus' Table," https://www.wycliffe.org /feast/10-lessons-from-jesus-table.
2. Verlon Fosner, *Dinner Church: Building Bridges by Baking Bread* (Franklin, TN: Seedbed Publishing, 2017), 17–24.

Chapter 13, Gospel Optimism

1. Sam Chan, *Evangelism in a Skeptical World: How to Make the Unbelievable News About Jesus More Believable* (Grand Rapids, MI: Zondervan Academic, 2018), 33–34.

Chapter 14, Asking Questions

1. Eric von Atzigen, "135 Questions Jesus Asked," https://mondaymorningre-view.wordpress.com/2010/05/14/137questionsjesusasked.
2. Alison Wood Brooks and Leslie K. John, "The Surprising Power of Questions," *Harvard Business Review* (May–June 2018), https://hbr.org/2018/05 /the-surprising-power-of-questions.

Chapter 15, Discipleship Rhythms

1. Mike Breen, *Building a Discipling Culture: How to Release a Missional Movement by Discipling People Like Jesus Did* (Greenville, SC: 3DM Publishing, 2016), 13–15.

Chapter 16, Social Transformation

1. Wikipedia's "Social ecological model" entry, https://en.wikipedia.org/wiki /Social_ecological_model.

Chapter 17, Loving People

1. Bob Goff, *Everybody Always: Becoming Love in a World Full of Setbacks and Difficult People* (Nashville, TN: Thomas Nelson, 2018), 3.
2. "Mosaic USA" from Experian, https://www.experian.com/assets/marketing -services/product-sheets/mosaic-usa.pdf.
3. "Mosaic USA Customer Segmentation Solution" from Experian, https:// www.experian.com/marketing-services/consumer-segmentation.
4. "Mission Impact: Ministry Applications for Mosaic Lifestyle Portraits" from MissionInsite, http://www.missioninsite.com/PDF_Files/Mission%20 Impact%20-%20Ministry%20Applications%20Final.pdf.

Chapter 20, Communication That Connects

1. Fred Guyette, "Jesus as Prophet, Priest, and King: John Wesley and the Renewal of an Ancient Tradition," *Wesleyan Theological Journal* 40, no. 2 (Fall 2005): 88–101; http://library.mibckerala.org/lms_frame/eBook/JESUS%20AS%20PROPHET,%20PRIEST,%20AND%20KING.pdf.

Chapter 21, New Wineskins

1. Alan Hirsch, *The Forgotten Ways: Reactivating Apostolic Movements* (Grand Rapids, MI: Brazos Press, 2006), 154–55.

Chapter 22, It All Starts with Identity

1. Gerald L. Sittser, *Resilient Faith: How the Early Christian "Third Way" Changed the World* (Grand Rapids, MI: Brazos Press, 2019), 97–115.

Chapter 24, Extended Family on Mission

1. Mike and Sally Breen, *Family on Mission: Integrating Discipleship into Our Everyday Lives* (Greenville, SC: 3DM Publishing, 2018), 30–31.

Chapter 25, What Is Church?

1. W. F. Moulton, A. S. Geden, and H. K. Moulton, *A Concordance to the Greek New Testament* (Edinburgh, Scotland: T & T Clark, 1978), 43.

Chapter 26, Why Small Groups?

1. Larry Osborne, *Sticky Church* (Grand Rapids, MI: Zondervan, 2008), 47–58.
2. W. F. Moulton, A. S. Geden, and H. K. Moulton, *A Concordance to the Greek Testament* (Edinburgh, Scotland: T & T Clark, 1978), 43.

Chapter 27, The Wisdom of Teams

1. Jon R. Katzenbach and Douglas K. Smith, *The Wisdom of Teams: Creating the High-Performance Organization* (Boston, MA: McKinsey & Company, Inc., 1993).

Chapter 29, Diversity and Alignment

1. Lauren Medina, Population Division, US Census Bureau, "Demographic Turning Points for the United States: Population Projections from 2020 to 2060," https://www.census.gov/content/dam/Census/newsroom/press-kits/2018/jsm/jsm-presentation-pop-projections.pdf.
2. Mark DeYmaz, *Leading a Healthy Multi-Ethnic Church: Seven Common Challenges and How to Overcome Them* (Grand Rapids, MI: Zondervan, 2010), 15.

Chapter 31, People Development

1. Reggie McNeal, *Missional Renaissance: Changing the Scorecard for the Church* (San Francisco, CA: Jossey-Bass, 2009), 89–108.

Chapter 33, Organizing for Ministry

1. Bruce L. Bugbee, *Network: The Right People, in the Right Places, for the Right Reasons, at the Right Time* (Grand Rapids, MI: Zondervan, 1994).

Chapter 35, Hard Conversations

1. Wikipedia's "Tuckman's stages of group development entry," https://en.wikipedia.org/wiki/Tuckman%27s_stages_of_group_development.

Chapter 39, Balancing Your Team

1. Alan Hirsch, *5Q: Reactivating the Original Intelligence and Capacity of the Body of Christ* (Columbia, 100 Movements, 2017), 3–17.

Chapter 45, Enjoy the Ride!

1. G. K. Chesterton, *Orthodoxy* (Cornwall, UK: Stratus Books, 2008), 109.
2. C. S. Lewis, *A Mind Awake: An Anthology of C. S. Lewis* (Boston, MA: Houghton Mifflin Harcourt, 2003), 24.

Chapter 48, Generativity

1. Wikipedia's "Generativity" entry, https://en.wikipedia.org/wiki/Generativity.
2. Søren Kierkegaard, *Journalen* JJ:167 (1843), *Søren Kierkegaards Skrifter*, Søren Kierkegaard Research Center, Copenhagen, 1997--, volume 18, page 306.

Chapter 51, Authentic Demonstration

1. Wikipedia's "Prayers of Jesus" entry, https://en.wikipedia.org/wiki/Prayers_of_Jesus.
2. "Septuagint Online," copyright ©2013 Joel Kalvesmaki, http://www.kalvesmaki.com/LXX/NTChart.htm.
3. Ellen Levy, "Gradual Release of Responsibility: I do, We do, You do" (copyright©2007 E.L. Achieve), retrieved August 18, 2020, from https://familiesaspartners.org/wp-content/uploads/I-do-You-do-We-do.pdf.

Chapter 53, Solitary Space

1. John Kirk, *The Mother of the Wesleys: A Biography* (Ambler, MA: Tresidder, 1864), vii. 38.

Chapter 54, Stay Humble

1. Chuck DeGroat, *When Narcissism Comes to Church: Healing Your Community from Emotional and Spiritual Abuse* (Downers Grove, IL: InterVarsity Press, 2020), 16–24.

Chapter 55, Intergenerational Engagement

1. Lucy Moore and Jane Leadbetter, *Messy Church: Fresh Ideas for Building a Christ-Centered Community* (Downers Grove, IL: InterVarsity Press, 2017).

Chapter 56, Recovering Broken Trust

1. Tom Nebel and Gary Rohrmayer, *Church Planting Landmines: Mistakes to Avoid in Years 2 through 10* (St. Charles, IL: Churchsmart Resources, 2005), 41–51.

Chapter 60, Staying on Mission

1. Roger Finke and Rodney Stark, *The Churching of America, 1776–2005: Winners and Losers in Our Religious Economy* (Piscataway, NJ: Rutgers University Press, 2005), 56.
2. Kevin G. Harney, *Organic Outreach for Churches* (Grand Rapids, MI: Zondervan, 2011), 79–116.

Epilogue: "Your Mission, Should You Decide to Accept It"

1. This phrase originates from the popular television series *Mission: Impossible* (1966–73); most episodes began with the team of special agents receiving a recorded message prefacing each new assignment with those words.
2. Philip Yancey, *Disappointment with God: Three Questions No One Asks Aloud* (Grand Rapids, MI: Zondervan, 1988), 121 and following.

SCRIPTURE INDEX*

*Key scripture passages are in *Italics*.

ABOUT THE AUTHOR

Ben Ingebretson began his ministry as a church planter in 1985 and has been working with church planters as a denominational planting director, trainer, and coach since 2001. He has developed regional planting efforts for the Reformed Church in America, The United Methodist Church, and the Moravian Church. His field experience includes Michigan; Florida; Chicagoland; Minnesota; and his much-loved home, the Dakotas.

Ben is the author of *Multiplication Moves: A Field Guide for Churches Planting Churches* and *Parent Church Landmines: Ten Mistakes Multiplying Churches Should Avoid*. He holds graduate degrees from Bethel Theological Seminary and Norwich University.

Ben lives in Grand Rapids, Michigan, with his wife, Karen. You may connect with Ben at beningebretson@gmail.com.